INSIGHT COMPACT GUIDE

SALBA

OXFORD

Compact Guide: Oxford is the ideal quick-reference guide to this ancient city. It tells you all you need to know about its attractions, from its glorious medieval colleges to the Ashmoleon Museum, from punting on the Cherwell to the gardens that inspired Lewis Carroll.

This is one of more than 100 titles in Insight Guides' series of pocket-sized, easy-to-use guidebooks edited for the independent-minded traveller. Compact Guides are in essence travel encyclopedias in miniature, designed to be comprehensive yet portable, as well as up-to-date and authoritative.

D0884976

Star Attractions

An instant reference to some of Oxford's most popular tourist attractions to help you on your way.

Sheldonian Theatre p17

Divinity School p16

Radcliffe Camera p19

St Mary the Virgin p20

Merton College p31

Christ Church College p41

Ashmolean Museum p49

Worcester College Garden p51

Blenheim Palace p58

River Thames p71

Magdalen College p

OXFORD

Introduction

Places

Culture

Leisure

Practical Information

Oxford – A Tale of Two Cities

Oxford is a secretive, inscrutable place, tucked away almost out of sight in the Thames Valley, in the gently rolling countryside of Middle England. It is famous as the 'city of dreaming spires', but these are hardly visible on approaches to the city. Tantalising glimpses might be obtained from the train as it finishes its journey from London, or from the western ring road, or as you descend past St Clements from the Headington roundabout. But for better views, you have to be on foot, admiring the skyline from South Parks or from the walk beside the river near Christ Church Meadow.

Queen's College detail

From whichever vantage point you choose, central Oxford is dominated by the buildings of the university. These make an impressive sight, particularly in the sunshine, when the spires, towers and college facades all radiate a golden glow. But ask a local where Pembroke College is and the chances are he won't be able to tell you. He probably won't be able to tell you very much about anything to do with the university, for this world-famous institution has always been an entity unto itself. Students come out on the town in the evening or can be seen in the Trinity (summer) term on their way to sit their exams, or rowing on the Thames, but life here is mainly played out within the cloistered confines of the colleges, whose battlemented gate-towers the townsfolk pass by, seemingly oblivious to the precious sanctums within. Oxford is a tale of two cities – of Town and Gown.

Students at exam time

5

Position and layout

Oxford lies some 50 miles (80km) west-northwest of London. The core of this city of some 100,000 inhabitants occupies a gravel terrace between the Upper River Thames (known in Oxford as the Isis) and the smaller River Cherwell (pronounced 'Charwell'). The first major settlement was established here in Saxon times, probably around the 8th-century abbey of St Frideswide on present-day St Aldates, and the original 'oxen ford' from which the town gets its name is thought to have been at Folly Bridge. The essential layout of Oxford dates from the later fortified settlement established by King Edward the Elder in AD901. The main roads that came in from the north, south, east and west converged at the central junction of Carfax – still the hub of the city today.

It wasn't just Edward the Elder who recognised Oxford's strategic importance on the natural frontier of the River Thames, but also later kings such as Henry I, who built a palace here, and even Charles I, who used it as his base during the Eng-

lish Civil War. As a glance at any general map will reveal, there are hardly any major towns in England further from the coast than Oxford. One assumes that this central location was also a major factor in attracting scholarly clerics from the Early Middle Ages onwards.

The origins of the university

Cloistered existence

Nobody knows when the university really started, but the first centres of learning were monasteries, notably St Frideswide's and Osney, established here by the Augustinians in the early 12th century. But, as was the case elsewhere in Europe, a need arose for higher training than the local ecclesiastical schools could provide. In 1167, during a feud between Henry II and the King of France, the University of Paris was closed to scholars and they came and settled in Oxford. The town was a natural magnet for scholars, who were attracted not only by the monasteries, but also by Henry I's royal palace of Beaumont. By the end of the 12th century an association of scholars under a *magister scholarium*, had been established, following a curriculum similar to the University of Paris.

In the 13th century, friars from the major religious orders went into the town to teach. In the beginning most students lived and studied like apprentices to their masters in large town houses or 'academic halls'. This system began to change in the latter half of the 13th century, when rich and powerful bishops established their own exclusive centres of scholarship in the town. The first colleges were born.

A venerable institution

Cherubs on Jesus College

Today, Oxford has 36 colleges, accommodating approximately 14,000 students. While the very appeal of the city is the medieval atmosphere of many of its college quadrangles, much has changed since the early days. In the 19th century, under the inspiration of men like Benjamin Jowett and John Ruskin, the university reformed itself from being a medieval, clerical institution based on privilege to a modern education establishment devoted to teaching and scholarship, with much greater emphasis on the teaching of science. But the colleges remain, as they always were, autonomous corporations with their own statutes.

Bodleian Library

The university is not just the sum of its colleges, however. Since the early days it has had its own central institutions. The Congregation (legislative body) of the university first convened in a special annex of St Mary's Church in 1320. Completed in 1478, the Divinity School was the university's first purpose-built faculty building. Libraries were important in Oxford from the very beginning, the first university library being established in St

Mary's church in the 14th century, followed by the purpose-built Duke Humphrey's Library, which developed into the world-famous Bodleian. Oxford is also home to the oldest museum in the world, the Ashmolean. The University Museum was founded in the mid-19th century and represented the arrival of the age of science. Though the Arts are still taught according to the age-old tutorial system in the colleges, the Sciences have their own purpose-built facilities.

University Museum

7

The university remains proud of its traditions. One of the most famous is the main honorary degree ceremony, the Encaenia, in June (*see picture, page 4*). The Chancellor of the University leads a procession of dignitaries and dons along Broad Street and into the Old Schools Quadrangle before conferring the degrees at the Sheldonian Theatre. The magnificent scarlet and pink robes they wear are a reminder of the days up until the Reformation when all members of the university were in holy orders. This applied to students, too, and their successors today are still required to wear their black and white subfusc garments while sitting their exams and receiving their degrees.

Oxford traditions

Town and Gown

The arrival of students in Oxford created friction with townspeople from the start. Tit-for-tat murders were commonplace. Back in 1209, for example, a local woman was killed by a scholar, and two of his unfortunate colleagues were hanged in revenge. The university went on strike and students fled in fear; some went to Cambridge where they founded Oxford's 'sister' university.

The problem was not just one of envy. As the colleges expanded, they simply usurped land occupied by the townsfolk and their businesses, filling the city centre with seats of learning. This led to large-scale poverty, a problem compounded by the migration of the cloth industry

to rural areas, and in 1349, the Black Death, which wiped out one-third of Oxford's population. Matters came to a head on St Scholastica's Day in 1355, when a brawl between scholars and the landlord of the Swindlestock Tavern at Carfax escalated into a full-blown riot. For three days academic halls were attacked by townsmen supported by a mob of thugs brought in from the countryside. Dozens of scholars died in this, the most notorious of many outbreaks of violence between Town and Gown. But the town paid the ultimate price by losing all its rights and privileges, and until these were reinstated by legislation in the 19th century its fortunes were almost entirely dictated by the university.

This was rough justice for a town that had seen more than four centuries of civic life before the university even arrived. Resentment continues to this day, partly as a result of the university's seeming reluctance to share its land and facilities with the town. There are also huge social divisions in Oxford: affluent North Oxford was spawned in the mid-19th century to house the dons of the expanding university; working-class Cowley was the creation of industry.

A class-conscious city

Gowns on the town

Economy and industry

The canal arrived in 1790, and the railway in 1844, but the town, hampered by the overriding presence of the university, didn't become part of mainstream industrial Britain until the early 20th century. William Morris (later Lord Nuffield) started his bicycle business in the High Street in 1893. In 1912 he progressed to designing cars, and within a year opened his first factory out at Cowley. Morris Motors was born, and Oxford, the city of history and learning, was transformed into an industrial centre. Although nowhere near as many cars are produced now as in the heyday of the 1970s, the present Rover Group, owned by BMW, remains one of the city's major employers.

But the university continues to exert a huge influence on the economic life of the city, and this is reflected in the nature of much new employment. The university's long traditions in scientific research have put Oxford at the leading edge in the development of medical and industrial technology.

Printing and publishing are almost as old as the university itself. The first book was printed in Oxford in 1478 and the city is now the second most important publishing centre in the UK, its activities spearheaded by the Oxford University Press, Blackwells and Heinemann.

Established by the early monasteries next to the Thames, the city's brewing trade went back even further than publishing; however, with the closure of the city's last independent brewery, Morrells, in 1999, that era is now over.

Oxford University Bookshop

Planning

The first time the town was given any say in local planning was with the establishment of the Paving Commission in 1771. Formed to direct the development of the city into the industrial age, the commission put an end to medieval Oxford, overseeing the destruction of anything that was regarded as an obstacle to progress, including town gates, churches, and street markets. The resulting accessibility of the town brought considerable economic benefits for local retailers, but there was a down side, clearly evident in the centre today. There can be no town in the world of similar size where all the major retailing is crammed into such a small space, principally Cornmarket Street and Queen Street. The university is partly to blame here: if colleges and university buildings hadn't obliterated many of the medieval streets, the pressure on the city centre today would be nowhere near as great.

Cornmarket Street

There have been various attempts to alleviate congestion in the centre, including one suggestion put forward in the 1930s for a link road between St Ebbes and the Plain, following the line of the Broad Walk across Christ Church Meadow. This particular scheme took more than 30 years to debate and was finally thrown out. Following repeated calls for the centre to be pedestrianised and for buses to be banished, Cornmarket Street and the western end of Broad Street finally became traffic-free zones in 1999, with other parts of the city, notably High Street, closed to through traffic during the day time. There are now also bus priority routes, closed to other traffic.

Pressure salesmanship

9

Even these radical changes have not solved all the problems: while pedestrians now have Cormarket Street to themselves, drivers complain about increased traffic congestion resulting from the new scheme. However, with more and more people using public transport and the excellent Park & Ride system, there may yet be a brighter outlook for the future.

Gardens

Paradoxically, it is the university that provides many of the urban open spaces in which citizens and visitors can relax and unwind. They include the University Parks, as well as the more intimate college gardens. Nurtured by Oxford's famously damp climate (the cause of much wheezing and coughing among the locals), the latter are oases of green right in the heart of the city. The best maintained are arguably the gardens of St John's College, while those at Worcester College are hard to beat for their fine landscaping. Magdalen College grounds stretch right to the River Cherwell, while the tiny Fellows Garden at Corpus Christi provides magnificent views of Christ Church Meadow.

Christ Church Meadow

Historical Highlights

1500BC onwards Bronze Age cattle herders and farmers build large round grave mounds on Port Meadow. During the Iron Age the landscape is dotted with small, mixed farms.

3rd century AD The Romans establish important potteries in the area.

cAD400 Migrants from Germany and Saxon mercenaries in the Roman army forcibly settle local farms; their descendants live as peaceable tenant farmers.

635 St Birinius, the Bishop of Dorchester, set out to convert the worshippers of the Saxon gods Thor and Wodan. The Thames emerges as an important frontier between two Anglo-Saxon kingdoms, Wessex and Mercia.

730 According to legend, Oxford's first abbey is founded by St Frideswide on the site of present-day Christ Church. This may have been the core of the original town.

912 First written reference to Oxford in the *Anglo-Saxon Chronicle* during the reign of King Edward the Elder, son of King Alfred, who fortifies the town to guard the river crossing into Wessex and protect the surrounding countryside against the Danes.

1071 Robert d'Oilly, Oxford's Norman governor, erects a castle to the west of town.

12th century Oxford attracts scholarly clerics from far and wide. Monasteries settle and bring prosperity and stability. The Thames provides power for the mills, and economy is based on cloth and leather as well as the various trades spawned by the emerging university.

1122 St Frideswide's Priory refounded by Augustinians on the same site.

1129 Osney Abbey built on an island in the west. It becomes one of the largest and most important Augustinian monasteries in England.

c1130 Henry I builds his Palace of Beaumont just outside the north gate, setting the seal on the town's rising importance.

1167 English scholars at the University of Paris are forced to leave and come to Oxford.

1199 King John grants the town his royal charter, and local government, based on the guilds, is free to develop independently.

1200 By this time an association of scholars has been established in the city.

13th century Friars form the various major orders teaching in Oxford. Their students live and work in academic halls dotted around the city. The first colleges are founded by powerful bishops; they are noted for their exclusivity and wealth and cater only to graduates.

1226–40 The city wall is extended and rebuilt.

1349 The Black Death kills one-third of the population.

1355 St Scholastica's Day. A pub brawl turns into a massacre of dozens of scholars. This event has dire consequences for the future of the Town.

1361 John Wycliffe, Master of Balliol, speaks out against corruption within the church. His teachings resonate throughout Europe.

1379 New College is founded as the first college to accept undergraduates. From now on the balance of learning in the town gradually shifts from the academic halls to the colleges.

1400 Oxford is one of the largest towns in England with a population of some 6,000. There are 1,500 students.

1426 Work begins on the Divinity School.

1478 First book (the Bible) printed in Oxford

1488 Duke Humphrey's Library opened.

1490s Erasmus and Thomas Moore in Oxford developing Humanist ideas.

1525 Cardinal Wolsey founds Cardinal College (later to be known as Christ Church) on the site of St Frideswide's Monastery.

1536 The university is brought to the brink of destruction by the Dissolution of the Monasteries, but Henry VIII saves the colleges by adopting them to train the state's most loyal supporters.

1542 Creation of the Diocese of Oxford, with its cathedral at Christ Church.

1555–6 The Protestant Martyrs, Latimer and Ridley, are burned at the stake in the city ditch (later Broad Street) on 16 October. Six months later, Thomas Cranmer suffers the same fate.

1558–1603 Reign of Elizabeth I. The city is transformed as a new civic pride emerges with increased trade and prosperity. The university expands greatly.

17th century Prosperity is fuelled by the famous glovers and cutlers of Oxford. University buildings begin to dominate the central area.

1602 Duke Humphrey's Library reopened to the public as the Bodleian Library.

1613 Work begins on the Old Schools Quadrangle extension to the Bodleian Library.

1621 The Physic Garden, later to become the Botanic Garden, established on the site of the old Jewish cemetery opposite Magdalen Tower.

1642–5 Civil War. Oxford is the royal capital and headquarters of the King's army.

1646 Oxford besieged by General Fairfax and his Parliamentary army. Charles I escapes in disguise and the city surrenders in 1646.

1650s A group of mathematicians and scientists, including Christopher Wren and Robert Boyle, meet regularly in Wadham College, before moving to London in 1658 to found the Royal Society.

1664–8 The Sheldonian Theatre, designed by Christopher Wren, is built.

1670s onwards Glove and cutlery industries in decline. But the university continues to provide new additions to the already famous Oxford skyline; many existing colleges are radically altered or rebuilt.

1679 Building of the (old) Ashmolean Museum on Broad Street, now the Museum of the History of Science.

1715 Hawksmoor's Clarendon Building completed for the Oxford University Press.

1748 The Radcliffe Camera built according to a design of James Gibbs.

1771 Paving Commission established. Much of old Oxford is destroyed to allow traffic easier access to the city centre.

1790 The Oxford Canal arrives from Coventry bringing cheap coal from the Midlands.

1830 The Oxford University Press moves to its present site on Walton Street. Suburb of Jericho built to house the Press workers.

1833 John Keble preaches his famous sermon on national apostasy, leading to the foundation of the Oxford Movement.

1844 A branch railway line reaches the city from Didcot.

1853 University Commission is established to reform the university.

1860 The University Museum opens.

1879 The first two women's colleges, Lady Margaret Hall and Somerville, open.

1913 William Morris establishes his car plant at Cowley. In the 1930s, as Lord Nuffield, he becomes the university's most celebrated benefactor in the fields of medicine and science.

1956 Creation of the Oxford green belt, checking the haphazard development around the city.

1960s Plans for a link road across Christ Church Meadow are abolished.

1996 Syrian-born businessman Wafic Said offers the university £20 million for the establishment of the Oxford Business School.

1999 Cornmarket Street is pedestrianised as part of a major new road scheme for the city centre.

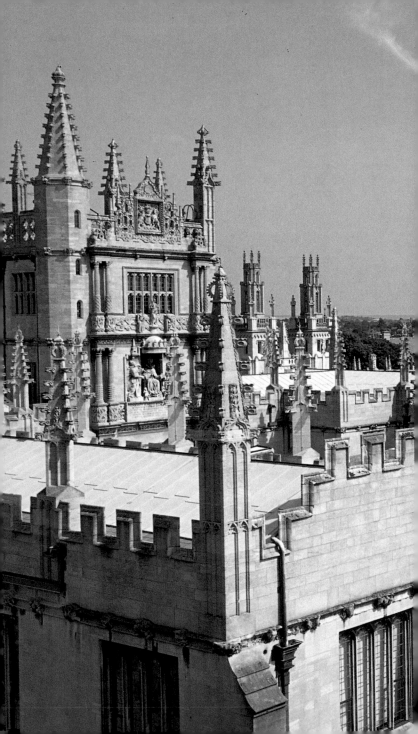

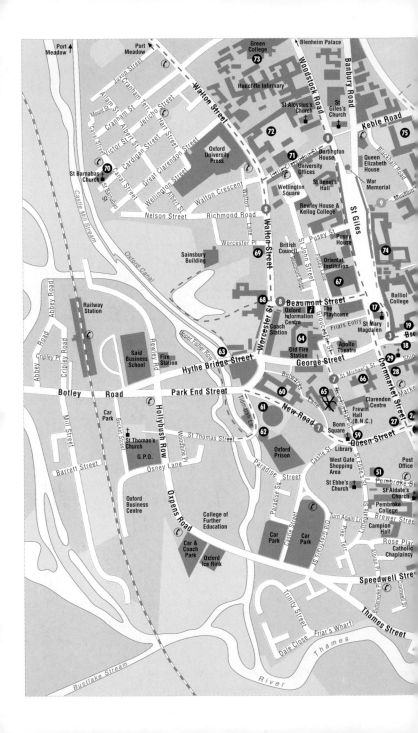

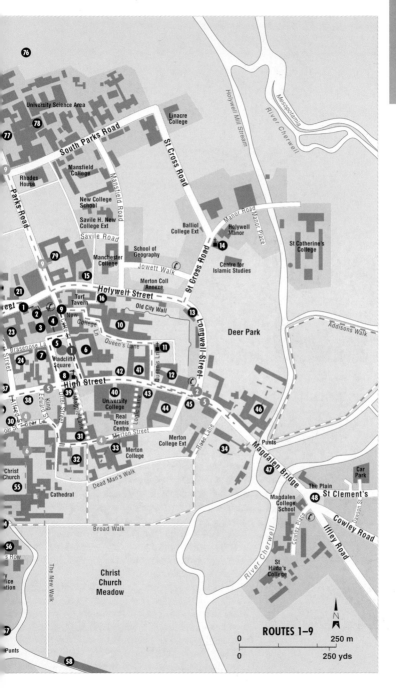

ROUTES 1–9

| 0 | | 250 m |
| 0 | | 250 yds |

Divinity School

Preceding pages: the heart of the University

Encaenia line-up below the Emperors' Heads

Route 1

The Heart of the University

Emperors' Heads – Sheldonian Theatre – Old Schools Quad – Radcliffe Camera – All Souls – Brasenose – St Mary the Virgin *See map, p14–15*

While the centre of the City of Oxford is usually defined as the busy crossroads of Carfax (*see page 29*), the university has no such focal point. Yet there is one area that, by virtue of the historic role of its buildings, can be described as the heart of the university. Lying between the High Street and Broad Street, it also represents one of the finest architectural ensembles in Europe.

At the eastern end of Broad Street, visitors are met by the intimidating gaze of the **Emperors' Heads** or 'Bearded Ones' which tower over the railings separating the street from the inner sanctum of the Sheldonian Theatre. Such busts were used to create boundaries in antiquity, but no one knows whom they represent. They were put up in 1669, the same year that the theatre was completed, but over the years their features eroded so much that they were no longer recognisable even as faces. Facelifts were performed by a local sculptor in 1970.

To the right is the Old Ashmolean Museum, the original home of the Ashmolean before it moved to Beaumont Street (*see page 50*). Designed by Thomas Wood and completed in 1683, it is considered one of the finest 17th-century houses in Oxford. It now contains the ★ **Museum of the History of Science** ❶ (Tuesday to Saturday noon–4pm) with a fine collection of astrolabes, quadrants, sundials, mathematical instruments, microscopes, clocks and, in the basement, various physical and chemical apparatus, including that used by Oxford scientists during World War II to prepare penicillin for large-scale production. Hanging in a corner is a blackboard used by Einstein in his first Oxford lecture on the theory of relativity, delivered on 16 May 1931.

The building to the left of the heads is Nicholas Hawksmoor's **Clarendon Building**, built to provide a permanent home for the Oxford University Press (previously housed in the Sheldonian) and completed in 1715. Around the roofline are James Thornhill's figures of the nine Muses. In 1830 the Press moved out of the Clarendon to its present abode in Walton Street, and the space is now used by the Bodleian Library.

Clarendon Building

Go through the gateway to the ★★ **Sheldonian Theatre** ❷ (Monday to Saturday 10am–12.30pm, 2–4.30pm; admission charge). Commissioned by Gilbert Sheldon, Chancellor of the University, in 1662, this was the very first architectural scheme of the young Christopher Wren, which he designed at the age of 30 while still a professor of astronomy. Modelled on a Roman theatre, but roofed over, the Sheldonian was built primarily as an assembly hall for university ceremonies, including the Encaenia, the bestowing of honorary degrees that takes place each June. But for most of the year, the Sheldonian is used for concerts and lectures, not the most comfortable of venues with its hard seats, but a magnificent interior nonetheless, spanned by a 70-ft (21-metre) wide flat ceiling, painted with a depiction of the *Triumph of Religion, Arts and Science over Envy, Hate and Malice*. The ceiling, with no intermediate supports, is held up by huge wooden trusses in the roof, details of which can be seen on the climb up to the **cupola**, which, though glassed in, provides fine ★ **views** over central Oxford.

Sheldonian Theatre

17

To the south of the Sheldonian lies the **Bodleian Library** (Monday to Friday 9am–4.45pm, Saturday 9am–12.30pm), which is entered through a small opening into Old Schools Quadrangle. Before admiring this beautiful courtyard in too much detail, first journey back in time by entering the doors behind the bronze statue of the Earl of Pembroke (a university chancellor) and proceeding through the vestibule into the much older ★★★ **Divinity School** ❸ (guided tours of the Divinity School, Convocation House and Duke Humphrey's Library, March to end of October Monday to Friday 10.30 and 11.30am, 2 and 3pm; Saturday 10.30 and 11.30am). Regarded by many as the finest interior in Oxford, work began on this central school of theology in 1426, following an appeal for funds by the university. Being the most important of all faculties, Divinity required a suitable space, but money kept running out

Old Schools Quadrangle, core of the Bodleian Library

and the room took almost 60 years to complete. Its crowning glory is the **lierne vaulted ceiling**, which was added in 1478, after the university received a gift from Thomas Kemp, Bishop of London. Completed by local mason William Orchard, the ceiling is adorned with sculpted figures and 455 carved bosses, many bearing the arms of benefactors.

Candidates for degrees of Bachelor and Doctor of Divinity were not the only people to demonstrate their dialectical skill under this glorious ceiling. It was here, too, that Latimer, Ridley and Cranmer were cross-examined by the Papal Commissioner in 1554, then condemned as Protestant heretics.

In around 1440, a substantial collection of manuscripts was donated to the university by Humphrey, Duke of Gloucester, the younger brother of Henry V. The walls of the Divinity School were built up to create a second storey for ★★ **Duke Humphrey's Library**. The library, with its magnificent beamed ceiling, was first opened to readers in 1488, but was defunct by 1550, largely as a result of neglect and the emergence of book printing (which rendered manuscripts redundant), but also due to the depredations of the King's Commissioners after the dissolution. It was while he was a student at Magdalen College that Thomas Bodley, became aware of this appalling state of affairs. Posted abroad as Ambassador to the Netherlands by Queen Elizabeth I, he used his far-reaching network of contacts to establish a new collection of some 2,000 books to restart the library. The room was restored and opened once more in 1602, and subsequently extended by the addition of the Arts End. Here, visitors can see original leather-bound books dating from the 17th century, some of them turned spine inwards so that chaining them to the shelves (a common practice) would cause less damage.

In 1610, an agreement was made whereby the library would receive a copy of every single book registered at Stationers' Hall. Soon, Bodley's collection had grown so large that a major extension was required, hence the ★★★ **Old Schools Quadrangle ❹**. Though only the cornerstone was laid before Bodley's death in 1613, this magnificent piece of architecture, designed in Jacobean-Gothic style, can be regarded as the culmination of his life's work. The quadrangle has a wonderful serenity, and despite being built much higher than college quads it is still light and airy. It was also built as the new home of the various schools of the university, and their names are indicated above the doors. Above these is the library space, but the continuity around the quad is broken at the east end by the splendid gate-tower or **Tower of the Five Orders**, so named because it is ornamented with columns and capi-

18

Duke Humphrey's Library

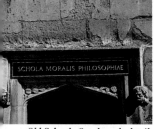

SCHOLA MORALIS PHILOSOPHIAE

Old Schools Quadrangle details

tals designed to provide students with an introduction to the five orders of classical architecture – Doric, Tuscan, Ionic, Corinthian and Composite. In a niche on the fourth storey is a statue of James I, the reigning monarch when the quadrangle was built.

The Bodleian Library has always been a reading library, from which no book could ever be borrowed. In 1645, even Charles I, desperately seeking a strategy to thwart the advancing Parliamentarians, was refused the loan of a book, and had to come in and consult one on the spot.

Leaving the quad through the southern arch, you come to the broad expanse of Radcliffe Square, dominated by the most familiar symbol of Oxford, the ★★ **Radcliffe Camera ❺** (closed to the public). Dr John Radcliffe, a famous Oxford physician, bequeathed the sum of £40,000 to found a library on his death in 1714. Based on an idea by Nicholas Hawksmoor, this purely Classical, circular building, surmounted by a dome, was ultimately designed by James Gibbs and completed in 1749. Absorbed as a reading room of the Bodleian in 1860, the building was just part of a grand 18th-century scheme to open up this part of the city as a public square, to replace the existing jumble of medieval houses. Not all the plan was realised, but it is amazing how the circular Radcliffe Camera appears to fit so naturally into the rectangular square.

Radcliffe Camera

The Radcliffe Camera is by no means the latest addition to the library. In 1930, the massive **New Bodleian Library** was opened on the other side of Broad Street to house the overspill. The new library is connected to the old one by a system of underground conveyors and shelves of books lie just a few feet beneath the surface of Radcliffe Square. The Bodleian not only has to cope with a constant flood of new book titles, but also every single newspaper and magazine published in the UK.

Out and about

To the east of the Radcliffe Camera is the gateway to the North Quadrangle of **All Souls College ❻** (usual entrance from High Street). Founded in 1438, this is the only college in Oxford never to admit any students, restricting membership to Fellows only and providing facilities for some of the best minds in the world to pursue their research. Much of the North Quad is the result of 18th-century alterations and additions, which came about after the medieval cloisters were levelled and a wealthy Fellow, Christopher Codrington, left much of his estate, including a large collection of books, to the college. The resulting **Codrington Library** (viewing only by special permission) occupies the building on the north side of the quad. Designed by Nicholas Hawksmoor, the exterior (the massive sundial is by Wren) is in Gothic style to mirror the

All Souls College

Brasenose College and Lane

Looking towards St Mary the Virgin

Historic coffee house

Convocation
Coffee House
OPEN
Morning Coffee
Lunches
Afternoon Tea

Entrance on
Radcliffe Square Side

View from the tower

chapel opposite, while the interior is purely Renaissance. The eastern edge of the quad is dominated by distinctive twin towers, also by Hawksmoor, while the southern side accommodates the 15th-century chapel, complete with original hammerbeam roof and a magnificent reredos behind the main altar.

At the other side of the square is the main entrance to **Brasenose College ❼**. The battlemented gate-tower and the ★ **Old Quad** behind it date from 1516, but the latter was altered a century later by the addition of attic rooms with dormer windows. The most distinctive feature of the quad is the sundial on the north wall. Looking back after crossing to the far side visitors are treated to one of the most startling ★★ **views** in Oxford, with the huge dome of the Radcliffe Camera looming above the entrance tower and the spire of St Mary's church to the right.

Brasenose is named after the 'brazen nose' door knocker that once hung on the gates of the academic hall that stood here before the college was founded in 1509. Moulded in the shape of a feline head, it dates from the 12th century and was said to protect students escaping from the law. Stolen from the hall and only recovered by the college in 1890, it can now be seen hanging in the **Hall**.

Immediately to the north of Brasenose, the narrow **Brasenose Lane** leads through to Turl Street and the Covered Market (*see Route 3, page 28*). The cobbled gully down the middle marks the line of the original open sewer.

The church of ★★ **St Mary the Virgin ❽**, with its soaring 13th-century spire, completes the harmony of Radcliffe square. It can be regarded as the original hub of the university, for it was here in the 13th century that the first university meetings and ceremonies were held, and all the administrative documents kept. Before entering via its north door, the visitor will see the sign to the ★ **Convocation Coffee House**. There can be few cafés with such a history as this, for it occupies the space of the former Convocation House, an annex built in 1320 specifically to house the University governing body, which continued to meet here until 1534 when the administration moved to Convocation House at the west end of the Divinity School. A library was installed above it, but this was later replaced by Duke Humphrey's Library.

Entering the vestibule from the north side, visitors can ascend the ★★★ **tower** (daily 9am–5pm, July to September 7pm; admission charge). The gangway at the base of the spire provides a magnificent view, revealing not only the layout of the city and many of the colleges, but just how much green space there is in the heart of Oxford.

Built in the 15th century, the **nave** is a fine example of the Perpendicular Gothic style, with slender, widely-

Catte Street panorama

spaced columns and large windows. In 1556, it was the scene of a major historical event, when Thomas Cranmer faced his persecutors for the last time. Having witnessed the deaths of Latimer and Ridley six months earlier, he was already a condemned man. But the Papal Commissioner now expected him to denounce the Reformation from a platform specially erected in the nave. Cranmer refused, instead retracting all the written recantations he had previously penned; he was dragged from the church and burned at the stake in Broad Street.

21

Almost 300 years later, the church was again the centre of controversy when, in 1833, John Keble preached his famous sermon on national apostasy. This led to the founding of the Oxford Movement which espoused a renewal of Roman Catholic thought within the Anglican Church and whose ideas were published in *90 Tracts for the Times* (1833–41). A leading Tractarian was John Newman, vicar of St Mary's, who ultimately converted to Catholicism and became a cardinal. Oxford remains a major centre of High Church Anglo-Catholicism today.

Gargoyle

Leave the church and venture round onto the High Street to study the main entrance of St Mary's, the ★★ **South Porch**. Built in 1637, with its twisted columns, broken pediment and extravagant ornamentation, the porch bears all the hallmarks of the Italian baroque, and was directly inspired by the canopy which had just been built by Bernini over the high altar of St Peter's church in Rome. Though out of style with the rest of the building, it is remarkable how well it blends in.

A guided tour

Return along Catte Street, looking back to admire Radcliffe Square. The view is at its most splendid from just opposite the Bridge of Sighs; the gateway to the Old Schools Quadrangle, the dome of the Radcliffe Camera and the spire of St Mary's together create one of the finest urban panoramas in Europe.

Route 2

The Northeastern Part of the Old Town

Bridge of Sighs – New College Lane – New College – Queen's Lane – St Edmund Hall – Longwall Street – St Cross Church – Holywell Street – King's Head *See map, p14–15*

Taking in the site of a pagan well, a Norman crypt, the medieval town walls and the birthplace of Morris Motors, this route covers sights whose origins span the entire history of Oxford.

Bridge of Sighs

The ★ **Bridge of Sighs** ❾, an anglicised version of the Venice original, which links the two parts of Hertford College, is the starting point of the route. Pass under the arch and into the dark and narrow New College Lane. This lane is the result of the replanning of the northeast quarter of town in the late 14th-century, when many early medieval dwellings were replaced by residential colleges. The original street pattern was obliterated, leaving New College Lane to wind its way between the high college walls.

Immediately on the left, a narrow opening between two houses, St Helen's Passage, leads through to the ★ **Turf Tavern**. Recently renovated, the Turf is a splendid low-beamed English tavern. Its foundations date to the 13th century, though most of the present building is 16th-century. At the back is an attractive beer garden, and along the alleyway at the front is another terraced area, tucked up against the exterior wall of New College cloisters, with braziers for keeping warm in winter.

Turf Tavern's beer garden

22

Edmund Halley lived here

Further along on the left, a plaque on a house wall indicates that this was once the home of astronomer **Edmund Halley** (1656–1742). Having calculated the orbit of the comet which now bears his name, and carried out many other scientific investigations, Halley was appointed Savilan professor at Oxford in 1703. He built an observatory at his home here, which is still visible on the roof.

The lane turns sharp right, between the cloister walls of New College on the left and the New College warden's barn on the right. Round another bend and straight ahead stands the gate-tower of ★★ **New College** ❿. Founded in 1379 by William of Wykeham, Bishop of Winchester, whose statue graces the right-hand niche, New College was the first college in Oxford to accept undergraduates. It was also purpose-built rather than built piecemeal like earlier colleges, and the design of the **Front Quadrangle** and surrounding buildings set a pattern that was followed by all subsequent college foundations.

New College Hall

The **Chapel**, to the left of the gate-tower, is a fine example of the English Perpendicular style, though the roof and reredos are 19th-century restorations. In the antechapel, beneath the great West Window by Sir Joshua Reynolds, is the dramatic statue of *Lazarus* by Jacob Epstein (1951). From the chapel, enter the ★★ **Cloisters**, the last part of the original college buildings to be completed (1400). Dominated by an ancient ilex in one corner, the cloisters have a serene atmosphere, and are largely unchanged since the time they were built; the original waggon roof covers the passage.

New College Cloisters

In the northwest corner of the Front Quad, steps lead up into the **Muniment Tower**, providing access to the **Hall**, where portraits above the high table include that of William Spooner. Elected warden in 1903, his habit of transposing the initial letters of words gave rise to many 'Spoonerisms' such as 'I'll damn you for sewage'. Outside again and through the archway is the **Garden Quad**, lined with 17th- and 18th-century college buildings and enclosed at the western end by a fine wrought-iron screen giving access to the ★★ **garden**. As well as a decorative mound, the garden contains a substantial stretch of the city's ★★ **medieval wall**, which dates from 1226 when the original timber defensive walls of the town were rebuilt. When the founder secured the land on which to build the college, he also accepted responsibility for the upkeep of this part of the city wall, and even now, every three years the wall is inspected by the Lord Mayor to ensure that this obligation is being fulfilled.

The garden and medieval wall

Exit New College and walk under the archway and round another bend into **Queen's Lane**. On the left, the otherwise featureless wall of New College is embellished by a string course of delightful ★ **animal sculptures**, created in the 1960s by Michael Groser. Beyond the sharp bend in the lane is the church of **St Peter in the East** ⑪, whose 11th-century tower is one of the oldest in Oxford. Originally dating from Saxon times, the present church is now the library of neighbouring St Edmund Hall, but visitors can gain access to the cavernous 11th-century ★★ **crypt**, one of the finest in Oxford, by asking for the key at St Edmund's porter's lodge. A gravestone in the churchyard commemorates James Sadler, described as the 'first English aeronaut', whose inaugural balloon flight took off from Christ Church Meadow on 4 October 1784.

Entrance to the crypt of St Peter in the East

Otherwise known as Teddy's, the diminutive **St Edmund Hall** ⑫ dates from around 1190. Regarded as the oldest surviving educational establishment in Oxford, it was founded as an academic hall by St Edmund of Abingdon. Fans of Pre-Raphaelite artists William Morris and Edward Burne-Jones should check with the lodge for per-

Church of St Cross

Holywell Street

Holywell Music Room

mission to see some of their stained-glass work in the chapel, together with original cartoon drawings.

The tranquillity of Queen's Lane comes to an abrupt end as it emerges onto the High Street. Turn left here and continue as far as the traffic lights, beyond which lies Magdalen College, with its famous tower (*see Route 5, page 37*). Turn left again into **Longwall Street**. Just around the first corner on the left is the building that housed the ★ **garage ⑬** in which William Morris built the prototype of the 'bullnose' Morris Oxford in 1912, a project that was to launch Morris on the road to fame and fortune and launch Oxford into the industrial era. It was only a year later that Morris built his car plant out at Cowley. Though the garage was converted to residential accommodation in 1981, there is an information window with further details on the career of Morris, the later Lord Nuffield (*See also Route 7, page 45*).

Adjacent is Holywell Street, but first continue north along the main road to the ★ **church of St Cross ⑭** on the right. The present church was founded in the 11th century on the site of an ancient chapel of St Peter in the East (*see page 23*) which was established beside a pagan Saxon holy well (hence 'Holywell'), and became an important place of pilgrimage. The only surviving Norman part of the church is the chancel, but the 13th-century tower has a fascinating feature, namely the **sundial clock**. The grave of Kenneth Grahame, author of *Wind in the Willows*, is in the churchyard. The key to the church is available from the porter of the neighbouring Holywell Manor; sadly, the ancient holy well is no longer there.

Cobbled ★ **Holywell Street** marks a clear boundary between cluttered Old Oxford and much later developments to the north. One of the most delightful streets in the city, it is lined by predominantly pastel-coloured 17th- and 18th-century houses as well as New College's imposing Holywell Buildings. Towards the end of the street, on the right, standing back from the road, is the **Holywell Music Room ⑮**, which was opened in 1748 and is said to be the world's oldest surviving concert hall. Regular recitals and chamber concerts are held here in an auditorium that seats 250.

Opposite the Music Room is ★ **Bath Place ⑯**, a narrow alley providing access to a ramshackle collection of old buildings, including the Bath Place Hotel with its excellent restaurant (*see page 68*) and, after a sharp turn, Turf Tavern. Holywell Street ends opposite the massive 1930s-style New Bodleian Library; on the corner is **The King's Arms**, a pub much frequented by students, particularly in June when they gather here to celebrate the end of their exams.

Route 3

Where Town Meets Gown

Martyrs' Memorial – Broad Street – Turl Street – Covered Market – Carfax – Cornmarket Street – Martyrs' Memorial *See map, p14–15*

This route straddles the boundaries between Town and Gown, highlighting the abiding contrast between life played out in the peaceful college quadrangles and the bustle of the busy city streets.

The route begins at the southern end of broad St Giles, where the **Martyrs' Memorial** ⓱ was erected in 1841–3 in memory of Bishops Latimer, Ridley and Cranmer. They were burned at the stake in the town's north ditch, now Broad Street, just around the corner, where a **cross** in the road opposite Balliol College marks the site of their execution. Latimer and Ridley went to the stake first, in 1555. Latimer offered the following words of comfort to his desperate colleague before both were consumed by the flames: 'Be of good comfort, Master Ridley, and play the man. We shall this day light such a candle, by God's grace, in England, as I trust shall never be put out.' He was right: the Catholic Queen Mary died three years later and the Church became permanently Protestant.

★★ **Broad Street** is aptly named, though it was originally known as Horsemongers Street after a horse fair held here just outside the city walls from 1235. Narrow at each end and wide in the middle, it has a feeling of spaciousness, emphasised by the grounds of Trinity College on the north side, which are separated from the street only by a wrought-iron gate. While the far end is dominated by the

Martyrs' Memorial

Broad Street

Sheldonian Theatre and Clarendon Building (*see Route 1*), much of the southern side of Broad Street is distinctive for its colourful facades rising above shops selling anything from antiquarian books to artists' materials. Here, too, is ★★ **The Oxford Story** ⑱ (April to October 9.30am–5pm, July and August 9am–6pm, November to March 10am–4.30pm; admission charge), a museum primarily devoted to the history of the university. After a brief introduction in a 'common room', visitors are propelled through the ages aboard a motorised medieval desk, experiencing the sights, sounds, smells, and above all personalities of this 800-year old institution, accompanied by head-set commentary (children's and foreign-language versions are available).

Balliol College

At the other side of the street is **Balliol College** ⑲, renowned for having produced a greater number of politicians and statesmen than any other college in Oxford. They include Lord Jenkins of Hillhead (present Chancellor of the University) as well as former prime ministers Harold Macmillan and Edward Heath. Together with University College and Merton, Balliol claims to be the oldest college in Oxford, said to have been founded in 1263 by John Balliol, as penance for insulting the Bishop of Durham. Little of the present college dates from this time, however, Balliol was rebuilt in Victorian times from wealth generated by its coal-rich estates in Northumbria. At that time, master of Balliol was Benjamin Jowett, famous for his liberal views and emphasis on academic excellence. But Balliol's progressive traditions stretch back much further than that: in 1361 John Wycliffe, Master of the college, spoke out against corruption and worldliness within the established church. His teachings resonated throughout Europe.

Adjacent to Balliol is **Trinity College** ⑳, which dates back to 1286, when monks from Durham Abbey founded a college on the site of the present-day Durham Quad. After the Dissolution, Sir Thomas Pope rescued the property and refounded the college in 1555. Unlike most other Oxford colleges, the Front Quad is not closed off from the street, and its lawn almost invites visitors to enter, which they do through a small entrance between the wrought-iron gate and a row of humble 17th-century **cottages** (rebuilt in 1969). Apart from the baroque **Chapel**, with its splendidly carved wooden panelling, stalls, screen, and reredos, the principal attraction of Trinity are its fine ★ **gardens**, entered through a wrought-iron screen from the Garden Quad. Extending all the way to Parks Road, they provide a wonderful feeling of spaciousness.

17th-century cottages at Trinity

Next to Trinity and right opposite the Sheldonian is **Blackwell's** ㉑, one of the world's most famous book shops. Opened in 1879 by Benjamin Henry Blackwell, the original shop was tiny, and even today the initial impres-

Blackwell's

sion is of an average-sized provincial bookshop. Downstairs, however, is the underground ★ **Norrington Room**, an enormous space stacked with shelves devoted to every topic under the sun. The pre-eminence of Blackwell's in Oxford is reflected not only here, but in other premises in the city, including the adjacent well-stocked Map and Travel shop, Blackwell's Too, a children's and family bookshop next door to the Oxford Story, and the Art Shop and Music Shop with its large selection of classical CDs situated just across the street.

Summer gadflies

Between the last two shops, shady **Turl Street** cuts through towards the High Street. 'The Turl' is thought to derive its name from a pedestrian turnstile or twirling gate set into the medieval wall that once ran along the southern side of present-day Broad Street. Today it forms a distinct boundary between Town and Gown, with most of the central colleges and the heart of the university lying to the east and the city's shops and markets to the west. The exception that proves the rule is **Jesus College ㉒**, a short way down on the right (west). Jesus is also known as the Welsh college because the money for its foundation in 1571 was provided by a Welshman called Hugh Price and much of its intake was from the grammar schools of Wales. The college retains its strong Welsh links, though two of its most famous alumni, Harold Wilson and T.E. Lawrence were non-Welsh. Commemorated by a bust in the chapel, the latter spent little time in the college, preferring to study medieval military architecture in a shed in the garden of his parents' house at No 2 Polstead Road in North Oxford.

Turl Street

27

Opposite Jesus College is ★ **Exeter College ㉓** (founded 1314), which is well worth a visit, particularly to admire the magnificent **Chapel** which dominates the first courtyard. This was built in 1854–60 to the design of Sir George Gilbert Scott and is almost a direct copy of the French High Gothic style as seen in Sainte Chapelle in Paris. The stained glass is magnificent, as is the mosaic work of the apse. To the right of the altar, visitors will also see the large tapestry of the *Adoration of the Magi*, made in 1890 to a design by Edward Burne-Jones, who had studied at Exeter together with William Morris. Another highlight is the **Fellows Garden**, beyond and to the rear of the front quad. The fine chestnut trees here were much enjoyed by J.R.R. Tolkien (1892–1973), author of *Lord of the Rings*, who was a student at Exeter and now lies buried in a North Oxford cemetery. He will also have enjoyed the magnificent ★★ **view** from the top of the garden wall, which provides a fresh perspective of Radcliffe Square (*see Route 1*).

Stained glass in Exeter's chapel

Further down on the left is **Lincoln College ㉔** (founded 1427), whose original front quad is all the more delightful because it has never experienced the kind of alterations and improvements undertaken by so many other, wealthier colleges. The Chapel Quad to the south was added in the early 17th century, and the chapel itself contains fine carved woodwork as well as exquisite stained glass by the prolific German artist Abraham von Linge, who arrived in Oxford in 1629 and proceeded to leave his mark on other college chapels as well, notably University and The Queens (*see Route 5*). During the 18th century, Lincoln College was a meeting place for the so-called Holy Club, which, under the leadership of John Wesley, grew into the great evangelical movement known as Methodism.

A ringside seat

Opposite shady Brasenose Lane (*see page 20*), Market Street leads westwards to arrive at the north entrance of the ★★★ **Covered Market 25**. Established by the Paving Commission in 1774 as a permanent home for the many stall holders cluttering the city streets, this is an Oxford institution that can't be missed. The central range is dominated by the butchers, whose fronts – particularly during the festive season – are hung with an astonishing variety of carcasses. There's also a high-class delicatessen and a pasta shop; shops selling sausages and meat pies, as well as cake shops and tea shops all vying for custom alongside smart boutiques and florists. The market wouldn't be the same without its traditional 'greasy spoon' café, but there also several more upmarket eateries selling baguettes and bagels, all providing instant escape from the bustle outside.

Golden Cross Yard

Inside the Covered Market

You can exit either onto High Street, or through an arcade and via the tastefully restored ★ **Golden Cross Yard 26**. Now equipped with a pizza restaurant, boutiques and shops selling organic products and herbal remedies, this

stands on the site of one of Oxford's oldest inns, where Shakespeare's plays are thought to have been performed on the cobbled yard.

Through an archway now and out into the rather less intimate atmosphere of central Oxford. Severely blemished by the wholesale destruction of many of its fine buildings, commercial **Cornmarket Street** – pedestrianised in 1999 – is the city's main shopping thoroughfare. Yet it does have its historic attractions. The busy crossroads at the southern end is known as **Carfax**, after the Norman *Quatre Vois* (four ways). This is the ancient heart of Saxon Oxford, where the four roads from north, south, east and west met.

On Cornmarket Street

Carfax still remains the focal point of the Town. Its prime attraction is the ★ **Carfax Tower** ㉗, all that remains of the 13th-century St Martin's Church which was pulled down as part of a road-widening scheme in 1896 and was itself built on the site of an earlier, late-Saxon church. The east side of the tower, which can be climbed for fine views of the city (late March to late October 10am–5.30pm, November to early March 10am–3.30pm; admission charge) is embellished with **quarterboys** which strike the bell every 15 minutes (replicas of those taken from the original church) as well as the original church clock. Also on Carfax stood the Swindlestock Tavern, where, on St Scholastica's Day (10 February) 1355, an argument between scholars and the landlord developed into a full-blown riot resulting in the deaths of many scholars. The site of the tavern is indicated by a plaque in the wall of the Abbey National Bank.

Carfax's quarterboys

Proceeding up Cornmarket, **No 3** is the site of the Crown Tavern, in which William Shakespeare reputedly stayed on his journeys between London and Stratford. Although changed almost beyond recognition in the 1920s, the **Painted Room** on the second floor (above the betting shop and open during office hours) has well-preserved Elizabethan wall paintings of fruits and flowers.

Continue until you get to the corner of Ship Street. Here the former **Ship Inn** ㉘, a fine medieval building, was restored by Jesus College before being taken over by Laura Ashley. Just opposite stands the oldest surviving stone structure in Oxford, the late-Saxon **tower** ㉙ of the church of **St Michael-at-the-Northgate**, which was built as a look-out against the Danes (April to October 10am–5pm, November to March 10am–4pm; admission charge). In the late 18th century the old north gate itself, part of the fortifications of Edward the Elder's original Saxon town, was dismantled by the Paving Commission.

St Michael's Saxon tower

Continue north past the Waterstones bookshop and into Magdalen Street, with the church of St Mary Magdalen on the right, to arrive back at the Martyrs' Memorial.

The view from Corpus Christi's Fellows Garden

Oriel College

Corpus Christi's sundial

Route 4

Quads, Meadows and Gardens

Carfax – Alfred Street – Corpus Christi – Merton College – Broad Walk – Botanic Gardens *See map, p14–15*

This route starts at Carfax and heads east, but soon forsakes the High Street to discover an old tavern and more venerable colleges before finishing at the Botanic Garden. Merton College is especially important, as many of its features provided the model for later college foundations.

From Carfax (*see page 29*), cross over to the south side of the High Street and proceed eastwards as far as Alfred Street. Turn right to arrive at one of Oxford's oldest pubs, the **Bear ③**, which dates from 1242. Its walls are lined with cabinets containing over 7,000 ties from a huge range of organisations, mostly clubs and regiments.

Walk due east from the Bear to arrive in Oriel Square. Founded in 1324, **Oriel College ③** is not open to the public, but visitors may be able to peek into the lavish, Jacobean-Gothic style Front Quad. Follow the road round to the left, into Merton Street. On the corner is the exit from Christ Church's Canterbury Quad (*see Route 6*).

To the right of Merton Street is the entrance to **Corpus Christi College ③**, founded by Richard Foxe, Bishop of Winchester, in 1517. Foxe intended the college to be a place of liberal education (hitherto unknown in Oxford), and he won praise from his humanist friend Erasmus for providing tuition in Greek as well as Latin. The college's most famous landmark is the ★★ **sundial** in the Front Quad, which is inscribed on a tall column topped by the college's emblem. But visitors should not leave withou also seeing the small college ★★ **garden** behind the Fellows Building. Dominated by a magnificent copper beech, the garden provides a fine view of Christ Church Meadow, with the Fellows Garden of Christ Church College in the foreground. The view from the raised platform at the back is even better, and you can see down into the secretive Deanery Garden of Christ Church, where Charles Dodgson, alias Lewis Carroll, first got to know young Alice (*see page 41*).

Beyond Corpus Christi, the street is dominated by the tower of Merton College Chapel. The gate-tower of ★★★ **Merton College** ⓧ itself is a little further along. Founded in 1264 by Walter de Merton, Lord Chancellor of England, Merton is one of the oldest colleges in Oxford. Like other early colleges, it was designed to be a highly exclusive institution, housing a small, privileged minority of mostly graduate fellows. The statue of John the Baptist (the patron) graces the central niche of the gate-tower, flanked by those of the founder and King Henry III.

Merton College

The Front Quad lacks the calm regularity of some other quads in the city. With buildings dating from the 13th to 19th centuries, it is typical of the piecemeal development of the early colleges. Nevertheless, Merton has some very special features that provided models for later foundations. Principal among these is the ★★ **Mob Quad**, reached by going through the arch to the right of the Hall and turning right. The oldest college quad in Oxford, its form is probably based on that of a medieval inn. The north and east ranges (for accommodation) were completed first, in 1311, followed by the south and west ranges, built to house the ★★ **Library**, the most perfect example of a medieval library in England (guided tours with the verger for a maximum of five people are available 2–4pm weekdays).

31

Mob Quad

The entrance is in the southwest corner of the Mob Quad, where the ancient oak door is believed to have been taken from Beaumont Palace, the Royal Palace of Henry I that once stood on Beaumont Street (*see page 50*). The library itself is up a flight of stone steps. Though its medieval structure remains intact, substantial alterations were carried out subsequent to its completion in 1379. The wooden ceiling, for example, is Tudor, while the panelling and plasterwork date from the late 16th and early 17th centuries. Among the many exhibits is one of the locked chests in which the manuscripts were originally stored. Books came later, as did the bookshelves, a feature introduced from Italy and Germany.

The west wing is adjoined by the **Max Beerbohm Room**, full of drawings by the famous caricaturist (1872–1956), who studied at Merton and wrote *Zuleika Dobson* (1912), a satire on Oxford undergraduate life.

The ★★ **Chapel** is definitely worth a visit. The choir (late 13th century) and transepts (14th–15th century) are, respectively, good examples of the English Decorated and Perpendicular architectural styles. It was originally intended to build a cathedral-like structure complete with nave, but this never came about, probably because of lack of funds and space. As a result the transept became the ante-chapel and the choir the chapel – another pattern that was to be repeated by later colleges. Attention is immediately drawn to the magnificent **east window**, which, with its fine tracery and original glass is easily the most beautiful in Oxford. Further highlights include a memorial, on the west wall, to Sir Thomas Bodley.

Merton marks its rowing achievements

Punting on the River Cherwell

Tropical conditions at the Botanic Garden

Exit Merton and retrace your steps to the left as far as the wrought-iron gateway (open daily until 7pm) leading along the attractive **Merton Grove** between Merton and Corpus Christi. A turnstile gateway at the end provides access to the broad expanse of Christ Church Meadow. Immediately on the left is **Deadman's Walk**, which follows the old city wall to the east. It was along this path that funerals once processed to the old Jewish cemetery, now the Botanic Garden (*see below*). It's possible to turn left here, but for better views continue south, past Christ Church Fellows' Garden, to the **Broad Walk**. To the right is the enormous neo-Gothic Meadow Building of Christ Church College (*see Route 6, page 41*), from where the delightful tree-lined **New Walk** provides a possible detour down past Christ Church Meadow to the River Thames and the College Boathouses. The main route, however, turns left along Broad Walk, taking in fine ★★ **views** of the college skyline to the north before arriving at an arm of the tranquil **River Cherwell**. Continue into Rose Lane and on the right is the side entrance to the ★★★ **Botanic Garden ㉞** (daily 9am–5pm, 4.30pm in winter).

Founded in 1621 by Henry Danvers, Earl of Danby, as a physic garden for the School of Medicine, this is the oldest Botanic Garden in Britain. Much of the original layout, based on beds devoted to the principal plant families, has survived, and the garden is surrounded on three sides by a 14-ft (4-m) wall, built by the first keeper, a German named Jacob Bobart. The fourth side is enclosed by laboratory buildings and the massive stone arch built as the main entrance in 1632. From the central pond, the ★★ **view** through the arch to Magdalen tower on the other side is magnificent. Visitors can also admire tropical plants kept in the massive **glasshouses** (daily 2–4pm) built next to the Cherwell. A stroll along the Cherwell here is very pleasant, the river crowded with punters in the summer.

Exit the gardens to arrive at the High Street, just opposite Magdalen College (*see Route 5*).

Route 5

Early morning on the High

Highlights of The High

Carfax – Magdalen Bridge *See map, p14–15*

High Street is different from other streets in central Oxford in that it is curved rather than straight. This is because the grid layout of the original Saxon town was out of alignment with the crossing point of the River Cherwell to the east, at the site of present-day Magdalen Bridge. So beyond the original east gate (where St Mary the Virgin now stands), the road, then nothing more than a track, began a gentle curve down to the river. Over the centuries, not only colleges but also inns and shops were built, endowing the curve with the grace and elegance we see today and inspiring Nikolaus Pevsner to describe the High as 'one of the world's greatest streets'.

Historically, the High Street was always busy. In the 18th and 19th centuries, the coach-and-four to London departed with ever increasing rapidity from coaching inns such as the Angel and the Mitre. Traffic congestion in the 20th century led to various attempts to limit the numbers of vehicles, including a (thankfully abandoned) scheme to construct a link road from St Ebbes across Christ Church Meadow, following the line of the Broad Walk (*see Route 4, page 32*). In 1999 the street was finally closed to general traffic– buses excepted – during the daytime.

The Carfax end is the commercial end, mostly taken up by shops and the occasional restaurant, as well as the long facade of the Covered Market (*see Route 3, page 28*). But there are interesting details which are worth examining. Starting on the south side, take a look at the sign above the silversmiths at No 131, a white dog with a giant

No 131's white dog

Kemp Hall

The Mitre

Rhodes Building

watch in its mouth. Just here, a small alley, one of many that delineated the original medieval plots along this part of the street, leads down to the Chequers Inn, a tavern dating from the 15th century. The next alley along is signposted to the Chiang Mai Kitchen, a Thai restaurant housed in ★ **Kemp Hall** ⑮. Built by an alderman in 1637, this is a fine example of the numerous timber-framed houses that sprang up all over Oxford during the great rebuilding of the city in the 16th and 17th centuries. The timber door with its projecting canopy is original, as are many of the windows; the interior is also very well preserved.

Back on the High Street, the next building of interest on this side is **No 126** ⑯. With its elegantly curved windows and fine proportions, this is the best preserved example of a 17th-century facade in Oxford. But the building itself actually dates back a lot further than this, for it is known to have been owned by a bell founder before being taken over by St Frideswide's Abbey in 1350. This is the story of many of the buildings along the High Street – medieval in origin but given new facades later.

Cross the road at the traffic lights to arrive at the ★ **Mitre** ⑰, now housing a restaurant and tearoom but once a popular student inn. It was built in about 1600 over a 13th-century vault, which sadly can no longer be visited. Nevertheless, the Mitre remains full of history, enlivened by anecdotes of ale-supping clergy. A sign in the lobby recalls its role as a coaching inn.

The Mitre stands on the corner of Turl Street (*see Route 3, page 27*), and on the opposite corner stands the former **All Saints Church**, now used as a library by Lincoln College. Beyond this is the High Street frontage to Brasenose College (*see Route 1, page 20*), which despite looking positively medieval was only built in the latter part of the 19th and early 20th centuries.

On the south side is a fine run of buildings with 18th-century facades, including the **Oxford University Press Bookshop** ⑱ at Nos 116–17, which sells only the books that the Press publishes. Further down, beyond King Edward Street, **Nos 106** and **107** (University of Oxford Shop and A-Plan Insurance) are particularly interesting. Together they were originally **Tackley's Inn**, built in 1320 and subsequently rented out for use as an academic hall (*see page 6*). A-Plan may allow you through to the back of their premises to see the 16th-century roof structure of the hall as well as a large medieval window. The cellar is the regarded as best medieval cellar in Oxford.

On the other side of Oriel Street, opposite the church of St Mary the Virgin (*see Route 1, page 20*), is the **Rhodes Building** ⑲ of Oriel College, built in 1910 from funds bequeathed by Cecil Rhodes, the South African statesman who made a fortune in Southern Africa after completing his education at Oriel and ultimately gave his name to Rhodesia (now Zimbabwe). Rhodes also endowed Rhodes Scholarships at Oxford, one of the most notable beneficiaries being Bill Clinton.

Continue along the south side, crossing Magpie Lane and past the Barclays Old Bank buildings. On the opposite side of the road is the High Street range of All Souls College (*see Route 1, page 19*). Dating from the 14th and 15th centuries, this is the oldest surviving part of the college, though it was refaced in the 19th century. A line of grotesque sculptures runs beneath the parapet.

Still on the south side, we now come to the long frontage of **University College** ⑩ (enquire at the porter's lodge for permission to enter). Claiming to be the oldest college in Oxford, 'Univ' is thought to have been founded in 1249 from funds left by William of Durham who had fled from Paris after a row between the kings of France and England. None of the original buildings remain, however, the college having been rebuilt from substantial benefactions in the 17th century. The range facing the High is in two parts, firstly the **Front Quad** (with main entrance), completed in the 1670s, and beyond the **Radcliffe Quad**, almost an exact copy completed 40 years later. The gate-towers contain, respectively, the statues of Queen Anne and Queen Mary. On the inner face of the front quad is a statue of James II, wearing a toga. This is one of only two statues in England of this unpopular Catholic king.

University College detail

Before reaching the main range, you may have noticed a small dome peeping above the wall. This covers the **monument to Percy Bysshe Shelley**, who was expelled after only six months at the college in 1811 for circulating a pamphlet on *The Necessity of Atheism*. The monument, depicting the naked body of the poet, who was drowned off Livorno in 1822, can be reached via a passageway in the northwest corner of the Front Quad. Another attraction of the college is the **Chapel**. Although refurbished by Sir George Gilbert Scott in 1862, it still retains its original, finely detailed stained glass, designed by the German artist Abraham von Linge.

As well as in Lincoln College (*see Route 3, page 28*), further examples of Linge's ★ **stained glass** can be found in the **Chapel** of **The Queen's College** ⑪ (access only with an official guided tour booked at the Tourist Information Centre, *see page 75*), whose magnificent baroque screen now dominates the northern side of the High Street. The statue under the little dome above the gate-house is that of Queen Caroline, who donated substantial funds to the rebuilding of Queen's in the 18th century. But the college is actually named after Queen Philippa, wife of Edward II, whose chaplain, Robert Eglesfeld, founded it

The Queen's College

in 1340. The chapel occupies the right side of the north range of the front quad, while the left side is given over to the hall, scene every December of the famous Boar's Head Feast, which commemorates a student who is said to have killed a wild boar by ramming a copy of Aristotle's works down its throat.

To the left of Queen's and directly opposite the gatehouse of University College's front quad stands a lone **sycamore tree ㊷**, whose presence endows the High Street with a rural flavour. As the only landmark that can be seen from both ends, it has long been regarded as Oxford's most significant tree and has even been described as one of the most important trees in Europe.

The High Street's famous sycamore tree

Continue along the south side of the High Street. Now the **Grand Café, No 84 ㊸**, with its elegant windows and Corinthian columns, was once the grocery shop belonging to Frank Cooper. It was here, in 1874, that Cooper began selling jars of surplus marmalade produced by his wife, Sarah Jane, from an old family recipe on her kitchen range. It proved so popular that a purpose-built factory had to be built on Park End Street. Although the firm sold out in 1974, the marmalade is still manufactured under the original label and sold all over the world. Next door, at **No 83**, are offices of the Oxford Bus Company, worth mentioning for the delightful first-floor Venetian window.

Examination Schools

Next comes the massive block of the **Examination Schools ㊹**, built in 1882 on the site of the Angel, one of Oxford's most important coaching inns (in 1831 it was operating 11 daily coach services to London and 13 others to all parts of the country). Introduced only in the late 18th century, the first written exams were held in the Divinity School, before moving to the various rooms of the Old Schools Quadrangle. But by the second half of the 19th century a new, purpose-built edifice was required. The building was designed by T.G. Jackson in the style of a Jacobean country house with Classical and Gothic elements. Students can be seen entering and leaving the building in the exam month of June, all dressed in subfusc garb without which they are not allowed to sit their exam. The High Street facade is impressive, but the most beautiful side of the building, with its fine courtyard, overlooks **Merton Street** around the corner.

Eastgate Hotel

On the same corner stands the **Eastgate Hotel ㊺**. It was at this point, in the middle of the street, that the east gate through the medieval town wall stood until its demolition at the hands of the Paving Commission in 1772. There has been an inn on this site since 1605, but the present hotel was built in 1899 in the style of a 17th-century town house.

Continue as far as the Longwall Street traffic lights (*see Route 2, page 24*), where you cross the road and proceed

towards Magdalen College, whose famous tower dominates the eastern end of the High Street.

Magdalen College

★★★ **Magdalen College** ⓪ (pronounced *maudlin*) was founded in 1458 by William Waynflete, Bishop of Winchester and Lord Chancellor of England under King Henry VI. It was built on the site of the Hospital of St John the Baptist, some of whose buildings still survive as part of the college's High Street range. Built outside the city walls, Magdalen had lots of space in which to expand, and its grounds encompass large areas of meadow, bounded in the east by the River Cherwell.

May Morning at the Bell Tower

Completed in 1505, the **Bell Tower** is famous for the Latin grace sung from the top by the choristers every May Morning. The tradition probably dates back to the tower's inauguration, but there were no loudspeakers in those days, and, one assumes, the crowds at the bottom were considerably smaller. When the singing finishes the bells ring out, sparking off a whole series of activities, including performances in the town by the Headington Morris Dancers.

During the Civil War, the tower was used as a vantage post by the Royalist forces who had established themselves in the city after the Battle of Edgehill in 1642. But while Magdalen, along with the rest of the university, lent its full support to Charles I, it did not support the unpopular James II, who attempted to make the college a Catholic seminary. In 1687 James briefly had his own man (Bishop Parker) installed as college President and had Mass, run by Jesuit appointees, set up in the chapel. With the advance of the Protestant William of Orange, however, James promptly did a U-turn and had the original Fellows reinstated on 25 October 1688, an event still celebrated in Magdalen as Restoration Day. But it was too late for the unfortunate king, who soon lost his crown and spent the rest of his life in exile in France.

Magdalen's Cloister

Deer Park

Magdalen College gargoyles

Enter the college via the porter's lodge on High Street and take the diagonal path across **St John's Quadrangle**. To the right of the **Founder's Tower**, a vaulted passageway provides access to the **Chapel** through a doorway on the right. Originally built in 1480, the chapel was completely redesigned in the early 18th century. But with its stone vaulting and ornamental screens, it is still worth seeing; the most interesting feature of the ante-chapel are the sepia stained-glass windows.

The passageway leads through to the delightful ★ **Cloister Quadrangle**, the 15th-century core of the college. With its vaulted passage, the quad still looks very ancient, though the north and east wings had to be rebuilt in the early 19th century after attempts were made to have the Cloisters cleared to make way for the **New Buildings**. Completed in 1733, the latter was intended to be part of a huge neoclassical quadrangle. Fortunately, the money ran out and only one range was ever built. It stands alone at the back of the college, reached by exiting the Cloisters via the tunnel in the north range.

Opposite the New Buildings, turn along the path to the left, where the massive **plane tree**, planted in 1801, is a direct descendant of a hybrid developed by Jacob Bobart in the Botanic Garden (*see Route 4, page 32*). To the north, beyond the fence, deer may be seen roaming in the **Magdalen Deer Park**. They have been here since the early 18th century, when they were introduced to supply the college with venison. Even today surplus animals are occasionally culled and served up in the hall.

In the other direction, cross the bridge over an arm of the Cherwell to follow the delightful ★★ **Addison's Walk**, a tree-lined path following a circular route of about a mile around the Cherwell's water meadows. At the far northeast corner of the walk, a bridge over the Cherwell

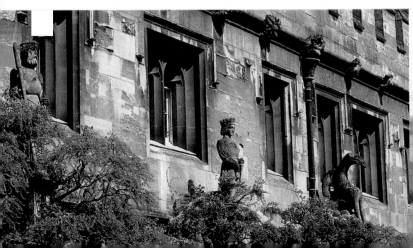

provides access to Magdalen's Fellows' Garden, demonstrating just how much space the college has at its disposal. The meadows and the banks support an abundance of flora, including the very rare purple and white snake's head fritillary, which blooms in the spring and grows wild in only a few places in Britain. But both the meadow and the groves of Addison's Walk are a delight at any time of year; on summer weekends, the Cherwell is busy with the traffic of punters who embark and alight at Magdalen Bridge.

Return to the entrance via the cloisters and then the **Chaplain's Quadrangle**. To the left, the Bell Tower soars heavenwards and to its right is the oldest bit of the college, part of the 13th-century hospital incorporated into the High Street range. Passing from the Chaplain's Quadrangle into St John's Quadrangle, you'll notice on the left wall an outside **pulpit**, from where a service is conducted once a year on the Feast of St John the Baptist (June 24), a tradition that dates back to the earliest days of the college.

Exit Magdalen, and on the opposite side of the street you'll see the main entrance to the Botanic Garden, incorporating the fine archway paid for by the founder, the Earl of Danby, which contains his statue as well as that of Charles II in the niche to the right and that of Charles I on the left (*see also Route 4, page 32*).

Continue along the north side of the street, past Magdalen's High Street range with its impressive array of **gargoyles**. Just beyond, steps lead down a landing stage, the main one in the city for visitors wishing to try their hand at punting (*see page 71*).

The first bridge to cross the Cherwell at this point was a timber construction built in 1004. It was replaced by a stone-built structure in the 16th century, but this was demolished during the Civil War and replaced with a drawbridge. The present **Magdalen Bridge** 47 dates from 1772. Part of the major programme of road improvements instigated by the Paving Commission, it has since been widened a couple of times to cope with the ever-increasing volume of traffic.

Magdalen Bridge

At the other side is **The Plain** 48, the busy traffic junction of the St Clements, Cowley and Iffley roads. In the middle stands the **Victoria Fountain** which was donated by the Morrells Brewery in 1899 and used as a drinking trough for horses. Until its destruction at the hands of the Paving Commission in 1772, the church of St Clements had stood on this site. The fine 18th-century house on the right is occupied by **St Hilda's College**, one of only two all-women colleges in Oxford, which enjoys fine views of the Cherwell and Christ Church Meadow.

Walk back across Magdalen Bridge for a superb view of the High Street.

Route 6

To the Origins of Oxford and Beyond

Carfax – Oxford Museum – Christ Church College – Pembroke College – Museum of Modern Art – Alice's Shop – Folly Bridge – Christ Church Meadow – University Boat Houses *See map, p14–15*

The neo-Jacobean Town Hall

Museum of Oxford

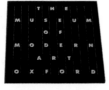

Museum of Modern Art

The road heading south from Carfax is called St Aldates. It was here, down towards the river, that the first Oxford settlement is thought to have been established, beside the Abbey of St Frideswide. St Frideswide's Abbey provided the core of the massive Christ Church College, part of whose rich folklore includes the tales told by one of its dons, Charles Dodgson, better known to the world as Lewis Carroll.

From Carfax, walk down the left-hand side of St Aldates. The building immediately on the left is the **Town Hall** **49**. Opened in 1897, this fine neo-Jacobean edifice was built to the greater glory of the City Council, reflecting Oxford's newly-found status and self confidence after it was declared a county borough in 1889. The Town Hall contains the city archives, and as Oxford was never bombed or burned the records are particularly complete.

Round the corner, in Blue Boar Lane, is the entrance to the former library, built at the same time as the Town Hall and now housing the ★★ **Museum of Oxford** **50**. (Tuesday to Friday 10am–4pm, Saturday 10am–5pm, Sunday noon–4am; admission charge). Displays inside highlight the history of the city from prehistoric times to the industrial age, with exhibits ranging from reconstructions of Roman kilns found at Headington to the legend of St Frideswide; from the origins of the university to the development of car production at Cowley. The most macabre exhibit is the skeleton of Giles Covington, an Oxford Freeman who was convicted of murder and executed in 1791.

At this point, fans of modern art should cross St Aldates and after the post office turn right into peaceful Pembroke Street. At the very end is the ★ **Museum of Modern Art** **51** (Tuesday to Sunday 11am–6pm, 9pm on Thursday; admission charge), which occupies an old brewery warehouse and mounts interesting exhibitions. The **Moma Café** is a good place to rest the legs. The church on the other side, **St Ebbe's**, is dedicated to a 12th-century Northumbrian abbess. The only truly ancient part of the building is the 12th-century doorway, the rest having been rebuilt in 1816.

Back now to St Aldates, where the eponymous evangelical church stands back from the main road, in leafy

Pembroke Square. The square also provides access, on its southern side, to **Pembroke College**. Visitors wishing to look around should first enquire at the porter's lodge. The college was founded in 1624 by King James I, and his statue occupies a niche in the tower of the Hall, built in 1848 but looking convincingly 15th-century. The Renaissance Chapel (1732) has a fine painted ceiling, as well as stained glass completed in 1900 by Charles Kempe, a former student. Another former student was the lexographer Samuel Johnson, who never completed his degree here but was awarded an honorary degree by the university in recognition of his achievements in compiling the first English dictionary.

Tom Tower

Opposite Pembroke Square looms the magnificent **Tom Tower** 52, built over the entrance to Christ Church College by Christopher Wren in 1681. Inside, the **Great Tom** bell chimes 101 times each evening (once for each member of the original foundation) at 9.05pm, Oxford being situated a stubborn five minutes west of Greenwich. Recast before being installed in the tower, the original bell came from the enormous Osney Abbey to the west of the town, which was completely destroyed at the Dissolution in 1536. The bell is named not after Thomas Wolsey, the founder of Christ Church, but after Thomas Becket, the archbishop of Canterbury brutally murdered by King Henry II's henchmen in 1170.

41

In the roof to the north of the tower are the rooms in which Charles Dodgson, alias Lewis Carroll, creator of *Alice's Adventures in Wonderland*, last resided while at Christ Church. Dodgson, a mathematics don at the college, made friends with Alice, the daughter of the Dean, while taking photographs of the cathedral from the deanery garden, and together they plunged into their own fantasy world (*see also Culture, page 64*).

Alice's Shop

Because there is no public access to Christ Church through the entrance under the Tom Tower, continue for the moment down the right-hand side of St Aldates to arrive at ★ **Alice's Shop** 53, which was drawn by Sir John Tenniel as 'the Old Sheep Shop' in *Through the Looking Glass*. The shop is devoted to the sale of souvenirs related to Alice. Directly opposite is a fine ★ **view** of Christ Church College and the cathedral rising beyond the **War Memorial Gardens** 54. The gardens provide impressive access to the public entrance to the college, through the **Meadow Building** (admission charge).

★★ **Christ Church College** 55 was founded as Cardinal College in 1525 by Thomas Wolsey, Henry VIII's all-powerful Lord Chancellor, on the site of a priory thought to have been founded by St Frideswide, the daughter of a Saxon nobleman, as long ago as AD730.

Christ Church

Christ Church from Memorial Gardens

Christ Church's Cloisters

The earliest Oxford settlement may have been a lay community serving St Frideswide's; Saxon tools, artefacts and items of clothing have been found during excavations in St Aldates.

But the first truly historical reference comes in a royal charter of Ethelred the Unready, compensating the community for the burning down of its church by the Danes in 1002. The priory was refounded by the Augustinians in the 12th century, and by the time Wolsey came along it had been greatly extended. Wolsey dissolved it, using the endowments to found his new college. But his grand scheme came to an end in 1529, when he fell from grace after failing to secure the speedy annulment of Henry VIII's marriage to Catherine of Aragon. Henry rescued the church and took over the college, refounding it as King Henry VIII's College in 1532. Ten years later, Oxford was made a diocese and the priory elevated to a cathedral, which Henry then combined with the college, renaming it Christ Church in 1546. Thus, the church here is unique in being both a college chapel and a cathedral.

Having entered Christ Church, follow the visitors trail through to the **Cloisters**, which date from the 15th century. Wolsey destroyed the west and south sides of the cloisters, as well as three bays of the priory church, to make way for the Tom Quad (*see below*). Through the first doorway on the right, the 13th-century Old Chapter House now houses a souvenir shop as well as a collection of cathedral and college treasures.

Enter the **Cathedral** via the next door on the right. The old priory church part of the Cathedral is rather disappointing from an architectural point of view. The aisles are too squat when compared to the size of the columns, and the small pairs of rounded arches fit too awkwardly into the main ones. By contrast, the 15th-century

★★ **Choir** with its lierne-vaulted ceiling is magnificent. To the north of the choir, is the reconstructed canopy from St Frideswide's tomb. The life of the saint is depicted in stained glass in the adjacent **Latin Chapel**. Designed in 1858 by Edward Burne-Jones, the dramatic scenes include a depiction of St Margaret's Well at Binsey (the 'Treacle Well' from *Alice's Adventures in Wonderland*). In 1877, Burne-Jones also designed the **St Catherine Window** next to the altar, depicting Edith Liddell, sister of Lewis Carroll's Alice, as the saint. The glass was made by William Morris; other works by these two Pre-Raphaelite artists are dotted throughout the Cathedral.

Burne-Jones window detail

Exiting the Cathedral by the same door, follow the cloisters round to the left, arriving, just before the opening to the Tom Quad, at the foot of the **staircase** to the Hall. Designed by James Wyatt in 1829, the stairs were built under the splendid fan-vaulted ceiling which had been created almost 200 years earlier, in 1640, by Dean Samuel Fell. The best view of the ceiling, and the single slender pillar supporting it, is from the top of the stairs. Across the landing is the entrance to the ★★ **Hall**. With its magnificent hammerbeam roof, this is easily the largest old hall in Oxford, representing the full splendour of the Tudor court. The walls are adorned with portraits of some of the college's alumni, including William Gladstone and Anthony Eden (two of the 13 prime ministers produced by Christ Church) as well as John Locke, the great philosopher, and William Penn, the founder of Pennsylvania. Above the High Table is a portrait of the college's second founder, Henry VIII. The portrait just inside the door is that of Charles Dodgson.

The staircase ceiling

43

Exit the hall and enter the vast **Tom Quad**. Measuring 264ft by 261ft, this is by far the largest quadrangle in the city. The whole of the south side, including the Hall and kitchens, and most of the east and west sides, were completed before the demise of Wolsey, who intended the entire quad to be cloistered (as can be seen from the arches in the stonework); the north range was only completed 130 years later. In the centre, in the pond, is a **statue of Mercury**, which was erected in 1928 to replace the one damaged by a student (the later Earl of Derby) in 1817. Beyond is the distinctive form of the **Tom Tower** (*see page 41*).

Tom Quad

Follow the eastern range of the quad to the northeastern corner where the **Deanery**, with its castellated parapet, faces onto the quad. It was here, during the Civil War, that Charles I resided when in the city. The south facade is embellished with a statue of the autocratic Dean John Fell, son of the Samuel Fell who designed the ceiling above the steps to the Hall. The Deanery Garden is just over the other side (*see Route 4, page 31*).

Christ Church custodian

Pass through the archway and enter the neoclassical **Peckwater Quad**, built in 1713 on the site of a medieval inn. The three enclosed sides of the quad are perfectly proportioned according to all the classical rules. Opposite stands the college Library (closed to the public), built in 1716 and originally designed with the ground floor as an open loggia. Its Corinthian columns lend weight and splendour to this side of the quadrangle.

From the Peckwater Quad, proceed to the Canterbury Quad. On the right is the entrance to the ★ **Picture Gallery** (Tuesday to Saturday 10.30am–1pm and 2–5.30pm, Sunday 2–5.30pm), which contains a small but important collection of Old Masters, including works by Tintoretto, Veronese and Van Dyck, as well as a famous Holbein portrait of Henry VIII. Visitors are obliged to leave the college via the Canterbury Quad exit, where they can link up with Route 4 (*see page 30*), or return to Carfax.

Folly Bridge

Because of the way the official route round Christ Church is organised, starting at the Meadow Building and finishing in Merton Lane, before entering visitors may first want to continue down St Aldates towards the River Thames. On the left-hand side of the road, a gateway leads to the University Music Faculty, with a sign indicating the ★ **Bate Collection of Musical Instruments** ⑤. Established from a donation by Philip Bate in 1963, the collection represents an unrivalled survey of European woodwind instruments, since added to by numerous donations of brass instruments, pianos, clavicords and harpsicords, as well as a fine gamelan from Indonesia (Monday to Friday 2–5pm, Saturday during term time 10am–noon).

Further down, with the redeveloped district of St Ebbes on the right, lies **Folly Bridge** ⑤, thought to be on the site of the first crossing point or 'oxen-ford' over the Thames created in the 8th century to serve the expanding Saxon community. Remains of a more substantial causeway (Grandpont), built here by the town's Norman governor, Robert d'Oilly, can be seen if you pass under the bridge in a boat. The present bridge dates from 1827.

Head of the River pub

From Folly Bridge, visitors can enter through the turnstile gate behind the **Head of the River** pub and walk along the Thames to the **College Boat Houses** ⑤. During the Trinity term in May, this is the scene of the Eights Week (*see page 65*). Apart from watching the boats, the walk along the river here is very pleasant. Just before the Boat Houses, near the confluence of the Cherwell and the Thames, the ★★ views across Christ Church Meadow, with the spires of Oxford in the background, are magnificent. It is possible to follow the Cherwell back to the Broad Walk, or alternatively walk directly to Christ Church along New Walk (*see also Route 4, page 32*)

Route 7

Along the Oxford Canal

To the West of the City Centre

Carfax – Nuffield College – Castle Mound – Fisher Row – Hythe Bridge Street – Gloucester Green – Carfax *See map, p14–15*

This route includes a journey into Oxford's industrial past. In medieval and later times the western part of the city, centred on the Castle Mill Stream, was crowded with wharves unloading cargo from the upper Thames. When the canal arrived from the Midlands in 1790, the area became a bustling inland port. Activity declined with the arrival of the railway in 1844, with the brewing industry one of the last to stop production in 1999.

Queen Street buskers

From Carfax walk along **Queen Street**, which is lined by chain stores and every bit as busy as Cornmarket Street, with the addition of buses nudging nose to tail through the crowds of shoppers. In the summer, some light relief is provided by **Bonn Square** ⑤⑨, named after Oxford's twin city in Germany, and a popular meeting place. On the opposite side of the road is the Westgate Shopping Centre, one of numerous ugly modern buildings erected in this part of the city centre during the 1970s.

On Bonn Square

Continue on into **New Road**, whose construction across the castle bailey in 1769 marked the beginning of local road improvements which were formalised by the creation of the Paving Commission two years later (*see page 9*). On the left you'll see the fortress-like facade of County Hall, the headquarters of Oxfordshire County Council, while down the hill on the right is the unmistakable spire of **Nuffield College** ⑥⓪. The site and funds for the college were donated to the university in 1937 by Lord Nuffield, otherwise known as William Richard Morris, who began life repairing bicycles in the High Street, progressed to designing the 'Bullnose' Morris in Longwall Street (*see Route 2, page 24*) and ended up by establishing the first ever mass production line for cheap cars out at Cowley (whose successor, Rover, continues to thrive). His manufacturing goals achieved, Nuffield was determined to use part of his vast fortune for good causes, including hospitals and charities. As far as the university was concerned, he had originally envisaged establishing a college specialising in engineering, but was persuaded instead to fund a post-graduate college devoted to the study of social, economic and political problems. Committed to providing a bridge between the academic and the non-academic worlds, Nuffield College has been the source of some major research developments in British social science.

Nuffield College

Attractive to some, plain ugly to others, the Stalinesque-style **tower** houses the college library. Only completed in 1960, the rest of the college is much like a Cotswold country house, with buildings grouped around two attractive courtyards in the pattern of traditional colleges. The lower courtyard was the site of the New Road wharves terminus of the Oxford Canal; some irony that the last vestiges of the canal trade should have been levelled by the pioneer of cheap motoring.

The green mound on the opposite side of the road is what remains of the **Castle ⑥** (closed to public), built by Robert d'Oilly, Oxford's Norman governor, in 1071. The mound was originally topped with a wooden keep (later rebuilt in stone), and the outer bailey was surrounded by a moat with water fed from the Thames used to power the castle mills – hence Castle Mill Stream. Many historic figures are associated with the castle. In 1142, Matilda (the Empress Maud) was holed up here for three months while

Quaking Bridge and Fisher Row

battling to gain the English throne after the death of her father, Henry I, in 1135. She escaped in the depths of winter down the frozen Thames, camouflaged against the snow in nothing but a white sheet, but the sad Matilda never became queen. From the mid-12th century, the castle was used to house prisoners, and although the fortifications were torn down after the Civil War, it remained the site of a prison. The present forbidding structure was built in the 19th century. The last public execution took place here in 1863; the last prisoner moved out in 1993 and there are now plans to turn it into a museum.

Continue along New Road until the next turning on the left, into Tidmarsh Street. At the end, the view is dominated by **St George's Tower** ⑫, which Robert d'Oilly built at the southern side of the castle bailey in 1074, above the chapel of St George. It was the Secular Canons of St George who established here what is regarded as the first learning establishment in Oxford.

Follow the road round to the right, across Quaking Bridge and into St Thomas's Street. On the opposite side of the road is the site of **Morrells Brewery**. Morrells, an independent, family-run concern, was the last brewery in Oxford, and its closure in 1999 marked the end of a long tradition. At one time, no less than 14 breweries thrived in this part of the city, drawing their water from wells deep beneath the Thames and using the river and canal for transportation. The first brewery here in Tidmarsh Lane was established as long ago as 1452 by the monks of neighbouring Osney Abbey (*see page 48*). The **Brewery Gate** pub next door to the brewery buildings might survive, but the brewery itself is slated for demolition to make way for a residential development.

47

Return to the Quaking Bridge. On the corner of **Fisher Row**, is the house lived in by Edward Tawney, who ran the Brewery prior to its takeover by the Morrell family in 1792. Follow the attractive Fisher Row along the Castle Mill Stream to the north, crossing Park End Street and continuing to Hythe Bridge Street and the present-day terminus of the **Oxford Canal**, where a sign headed ★ **Oxford Canal Walk** ⑬ indicates the distances to towns further up the waterway. While visitors might find the 83 miles to Coventry somewhat ambitious, a short walk here along the canal towpath, overhung by trees in the summer and lined with colourful narrowboats, is well worthwhile. While some boats are only temporarily moored, others have flower pots and wheelbarrows on their roofs indicating a more permanent stay. The canal runs along the back of Worcester College (*see Route 8, page 51*), past the district of Jericho and then Lucy's Ironworks, where steps up to the bridge provide access to Port Meadow (*see page 57*).

On the Oxford Canal

Passing Lucy's Ironworks

Back at Hythe Bridge, Hythe Bridge Street leads westwards past a number of restaurants, merging with Botley Road near the new Said Business School and the railway station. If you continue under the railway line, keeping to the south side of Botley Road, a bridge built in 1888 leads onto **Osney Island**, which is surrounded by arms of the River Thames. The district has nicely preserved 1850s terraces and characterful waterside pubs, and in the summer the river is busy with narrow boats and cruisers. It is difficult to imagine today, but back in the Middle Ages, the whole island was occupied by one of the largest Augustinian monasteries in England. Founded in 1129, but destroyed at the Dissolution, Osney Abbey was among the first major centres of learning in Oxford. It's bell was recast as the Great Tom bell, which still chimes in Christ Church College *(see Route 6, page xx)*.

Gloucester Green mural and café

The main route continues towards the city along Hythe Bridge Street. Cross the road at the traffic lights and go left up the hill, before turning right into **Gloucester Green ⑥**, a large pedestrianised shopping square opened in 1989. Before you get into the main square, look out for the Old School House, which now houses the city's **Tourist Information Centre**, where leaflets can be obtained as well as bookings made for guided walking tours *(see Facts for the Visitor, page 75)*. The square itself is surrounded by a variety of shops and eating places and is the scene of a market every Wednesday, and an antiques and crafts market every Thursday.

Leave Gloucester Green passing the MGM cinema and soon turn right into **New Inn Hall Street**. The original New Inn Hall, a medieval academic hall, has gone, its place taken by **St Peter's College ⑥**, which was founded in 1929 and lines the right-hand side of the street. The entrance to the college is through Linton House, the first headquarters of the Oxford Canal Company, dating from 1797. The chapel of the college is the church of Peter-le-Bailey; rebuilt in the 18th century, it occupies the same site as the original Norman church.

On the opposite side of the road, St Michael's Street leads back towards Cornmarket Street. Off it is the entrance to the **Oxford Union ⑥** (closed to the public), the great university debating forum, where famous public figures are invited to address the assembled students. But continue along New Inn Hall Street, where, next to the entrance to Frewin Hall, a plaque indicates a house that was the first Methodist meeting house in Oxford, used for the first time in 1783, eight years before the death of John Wesley, who had founded the movement while at Lincoln College *(see Route 3, page 28)*.

Continue along to Bonn Square and back to Carfax.

Route 8

Ashmolean Museum

Famous Institutions

Martyrs' Memorial – Ashmolean Museum – Worcester College – Oxford University Press – Little Clarendon Street – St Giles *See map, p14–15*

This route begins by exploring past civilisations in the Ashmolean Museum before entering the district of Jericho to discover the city's publishing heritage. Publishing remains the theme as we return to St Giles, where the Eagle and Child pub was a meeting place of some famous authors.

Looking across from the Martyrs' Memorial, the entrance to Beaumont Street is dominated on the left by the famous **Randolph Hotel**, a splendid Victorian-Gothic edifice dating from 1863, and on the right by the neo-Grecian facade of the **Taylor Institute**. The four statues standing on the tops of the columns represent France, Germany, Italy and Spain, for the institute was founded for the study of the languages of these four countries.

Randolph Hotel

The Taylor Institute forms the east wing of the giant ★★★ **Ashmolean Museum** (Tuesday to Saturday 10am–5pm, Sunday 2–5pm, Bank Holiday Mondays 2–5pm), whose main facade stretches along the north side of Beaumont Street. Built in 1841–5 and containing the University of Oxford's collections of art and antiquities, the Ashmolean is the oldest museum in the country. Set up by the antiquary and scholar Elias Ashmole in 1683, its first home was in purpose-built premises on Broad Street (now the Museum of the History of Science, *see Route 1, page 16*). But the origin of the collection goes back to before Ashmole's day, and not to Oxford, but to

Alfred Jewel

'The Hunt in the Forest'

On Beaumont Street

Lambeth, London. There, in a pub called The Ark, the early 17th-century naturalist and royal gardener John Tradescant displayed his extensive collection of rarities and curiosities either gathered by himself on his trips to Europe or given to him by sea captains. After his death in 1638, Tradescant's son, also called John, infused the collection with items from the New World, specifically Virginia, to which he travelled on several occasions. The collection was ultimately bequeathed to Ashmole, who then presented it to the university. Items from the original 'Ark' can still be seen today in the museum, in the special **Tradescant Room** on the first floor. They include a rhinoceros-horn cup from China, Henry VIII's stirrups and hawking gear, and, as the star attraction, ★★ **Powhattan's Mantle**. Powhattan was the king of Virginia, and as any child will tell you, the father of Pocahontas.

Since moving to Beaumont Street, the Ashmolean has developed into one of the world's great museums. The Antiquities Department has a fine Egyptian section, and extensive displays covering Ancient Greece (particularly vases), Rome and the Near East, as well as Dark-Age Europe and Anglo-Saxon Britain. It is in the latter section (in the Leeds Room on the first floor, No 32) that the museum's most famous artefact is to be found, namely the ★★★ **Alfred Jewel**. Found in Somerset in 1693, it is regarded as the finest piece of Saxon art ever discovered. Consisting of an enamel seated figure set under a rock crystal in a gold frame bearing the inscription *Aelfred mec heht gewyrcan* ('Alfred had me made'), it isn't in fact an item of personal jewellery but would have been affixed to a pointer used for following the text in a manuscript.

The Department of Eastern Art, which includes some superb examples of Gandharan sculpture, is also impressive, but the other main attraction of the museum is the Department of Western Art on the first floor, which includes drawings by Michelangelo and Raphael, as well as *The Hunt in the Forest*, painted by the Florentine artist Paolo Uccello in 1466. The Heberden Coin Room, also on the first floor, contains an interesting collection of coins and medals.

Since renovations carried out in 1995, the public entrance to the museum is no longer through the large blue doors in the centre, but through doors into the west wing. The renovations included the provision of a pleasant café in the vaulted basement, which can also be reached directly from the outside.

Leaving the Ashmolean, turn right along **Beaumont Street**. Now lined by terraces of fine Regency houses, the western end of this street was once occupied by Beaumont Palace, built in the early 12th century by Henry I as his royal residence in Oxford and the birthplace of his sons Richard (the Lionheart) and John. Though the palace represented the town's rise in importance during the early Middle Ages, it didn't remain here for long; the original door was used by the founders of Merton as their library entrance, where it can still be seen today (*see page 31*).

At the end of Beaumont Street, cross the road to enter ★★ **Worcester College** ❻❽. Worcester is different from most other colleges in that it has no intimate, enclosed quadrangles. But this in no way detracts from the appeal of the place, for as well as some fine architecture, the college boasts beautiful gardens. Founded in the early 18th century, the origins of the college go back to Gloucester Hall, which was established on the site for Benedictine monks in 1283, but dissolved in about 1539.

Worcester College's medieval cottages

Revival only came at the end of the 17th century with funds provided by Sir Thomas Cookes, a Worcestershire baronet. The new Worcester College received its statutes in 1714, but the 18th-century building programme was financed by another man, George Clarke, regarded as the college's second founder. Despite this infusion of money, Worcester was never very wealthy, and the original Gloucester Hall ★ **medieval cottages** owe their survival to the fact that the college could only afford the two neoclassical ranges we see today. Of these, the front or west range is the most interesting, for it contains the **Library** (above the cloister), the **Hall** and the **Chapel** (in the two wings). Designed by Nicholas Hawksmoor, the library was founded on a substantial collection of books and manuscripts donated by George Clarke and includes a large proportion of the surviving drawings of Inigo Jones. The hall and chapel were completed by James Wyatt in the 1770s, but the hall received its present Raphaelesque countenance at the hands of William Burges in 1864.

51

Worcester is sited on a slope, the land dropping away to the west. A tunnel at the end of the Gloucester Hall cottages leads through to the ★★ **gardens**, which are as beautiful as any in Oxford, a fact endorsed by Lewis Carroll in *Alice's Adventures in Wonderland* when he describes the tunnel 'not much larger than a rathole' leading 'to the loveliest garden you ever saw'.

'The loveliest garden you ever saw'

Landscaped like a small park, the gardens are planted with magnificent trees and shrubs and include a lovely willow-fringed lake. They were laid out in the early 19th century after the completion of the Oxford Canal (1790) which now forms the western boundary of the college grounds. A walk around the lake is highly recommended. Looking back through the trees there are glimpses of the magnificent Palladian facade of the **Provost's House**, while at the northern end of the lake is the 1982 ★ **Sainsbury**

Sainsbury Building

Walton Street gallery and house facade

Building. Regarded as one of the best pieces of modern architecture in Oxford, its carefully juxtaposed roof lines and walls descend to a delightful lakeside terrace. The college playing fields stretch away to the north.

Exit Worcester and walk north along **Walton Street**. On the corner of Worcester Place stands **Ruskin College ⑥⑨**, one of a number of institutions founded in memory of the art and later social critic, John Ruskin, for the education of working men and women. To the south, the district of **Jericho** was developed in the early 18th century to house the increasing numbers of workers in this part of the city after the arrival of the Oxford Canal in 1790. When the **Oxford University Press** (situated in a grand neoclassical building just round the first corner) moved here from the Clarendon Building in 1830, further houses were built to accommodate the print workers. And it was the print workers who made up the majority of the congregation of the massive **church of St Barnabas ⑦⓪**, which was built by the canal in 1868 and whose Italianate tower dominates the district.

Featured as the cholera-ridden slum of Beersheba in Thomas Hardy's *Jude the Obscure*, Jericho's working-class credentials have long expired, for its prime location at the threshold to the city has made it a desirable area to live, particularly for wealthy students and young professionals. House prices have soared and Walton Street is now lined with craft shops, boutiques, delicatessens and restaurants. Opposite the Press building is the neo-Grecian facade of the old St Paul's church, built in 1936. It no longer serves as a church today but as **Freuds**, a wine bar and restaurant with live-music programmes specialising in jazz.

If you continue along Walton Street, past the **Phoenix Picture House** and Raymond Blanc's brasserie, **Le Petit Blanc**, you'll get to Walton Well Road, which leads over the canal and railway line to Port Meadow (*see page 57*). Otherwise, retrace your steps to **Little Clarendon Street** ❼❶, which links Walton Street with St Giles. Amongst various administrative buildings of the university, bars, brasseries and cafés lie cheek by jowl with boutiques and gift shops, including **Tumi** selling Latin American crafts and music.

*For Latin
American crafts*

Now enter the Woodstock Road end of St Giles. Immediately on the left is Maison Blanc, a wonderful patisserie, and adjacent to that is **Browns**, a long established restaurant whose reputation is not only based on good food but also on its child-friendly attitude.

If you continue northwards along the Woodstock Road, just after the church of St Aloysius is the entrance to **Somerville College** ❼❷, which though founded in 1859, was not – in common with the other four women's halls founded in the late 19th century – recognised as a full college until 1959. Despite this handicap, Somerville has educated an extraordinary number of female public figures, including Margaret Thatcher and Indira Gandhi.

Old girl Margaret Thatcher

Former British Prime Minister, Margaret Thatcher, was a student at Somerville College

53

Further along Woodstock Road, after the Radcliffe Infirmary, Green College was only founded in 1979. Unfortunately, the famous **Radcliffe Observatory** ❼❸, designed by James Wyatt and completed in 1794, has been absorbed into the college and cannot generally be visited by the public. Also off limits is the attractive physic garden at its base, though information about both can be obtained at the porter's lodge.

Return down Woodstock Road into **St Giles**. This broad boulevard runs between the War Memorial and St Giles' church in the north to the Martyrs' Memorial in the south. The right-hand side (west) of St Giles is lined with a series of attractive 17th- and 18th-century houses, some housing a variety of religious institutions, including the Christian Scientists at Nos 34–6, St Benet's Hall for Benedictine monks at No 38 and the Quakers at No 43. Beyond Pusey Street, St Cross College is an Anglican theological college. But perhaps the most interesting building on this side of St Giles is the **Eagle and Child** pub, on the corner of Wellington Place. It has been an inn since at least 1650, but its fame rests on the literary group known as the Inklings which met up here in a back room between 1939 and 1962. Headed by C.S. Lewis, the group included such luminaries as J.R.R. Tolkien and Charles Williams (*see page 64*).

Eagle and Child

For two days every September (the Monday and Tuesday following the first Sunday of the month) St Giles is the scene of the St Giles Fair. Cherished by people of all ages and backgrounds, the origins of this colourful fair date back to a parish wake first recorded in 1624.

Continue down St Giles to the Martyrs' Memorial.

Route 9

The Old and the Not so Old

Martyrs' Memorial – St John's College – Keble College – University Parks – University Museum – Pitt Rivers Museum – Broad Street *See map, p14–15*

Starting in St Giles, this route explores the area immediately to the north of the city centre, which was developed after the great university reforms in the mid-19th century, and includes two wonderful museums.

St John's College: Charles I and Canterbury Quad

From the Martyrs' Memorial, follow the east side of St Giles to the entrance of ★★ **St John's College** ⓴. Founded in 1457 for Cistercian monks and originally named after St Bernard, the college was refounded after the Dissolution by Sir Thomas White, who was a member of the wealthy Merchant Taylor's guild, and renamed St John's after the patron saint of tailors. It remains one of the richest colleges in Oxford.

The niche on the gate-tower is occupied by St Bernard while that on the inner side of the tower contains a superb modern statue of St John the Baptist, created by Eric Gill in 1936. Apart from this addition, most of the Front Quad dates to the time of the college's foundation. But passing through the archway to the east, the visitor jumps two centuries into the magnificent ★★ **Canterbury Quad**. Built by the little-known architect Adam Browne, this magnificent baroque quadrangle was financed by Archbishop Laud, famous as the university chancellor responsible for drawing up stringent rules governing the behaviour and dress of scholars, which remained in force until more progressive ideologies took over in the 1850s.

Straight ahead, flanked by a fine Tuscan-style arcade, a two-storey portal contains a bronze statue of Charles I. He faces a similar statue of his wife, Queen Henrietta Maria, housed in a niche on the opposite side. When the quad was completed in 1636, both were invited to attend the opening ceremony, which is said to have cost more than the buildings themselves.

St John's gardens

Beyond the quad, the archway leads through to the ★★ **gardens**. Like neighbouring Trinity College (*see Route 3, page 26*), St John's was built outside the city walls and so the gardens are very spacious. The path around the lawn twists and turns between carefully tended shrubs and groves of trees, providing a wonderful blend of the formal and the naturalistic. Visitors can extend their walk by taking a side path to the north, past rockeries and shady lawns, catching glimpses of more modern college buildings to the north.

Exit the college and turn right. At the **Lamb and Flag** pub, a passageway transports the visitor from the Middle Ages to the 19th century, emerging as it does onto Parks Road, which was first laid out in the 1830s. Directly opposite stands the mighty neo-Gothic facade of the University Museum. But before crossing the road, turn left to arrive at the enormous brick edifice that is **Keble College** 75. Founded in 1868 as a memorial to John Keble, the inspirer of the Oxford Movement (*see page 21*), the college was created as bastion of High Church traditionalism at a time when the rest of the university was undergoing massive liberalising reforms. Initially students had to lead an almost monastic life of poverty and obedience. The Tractarian founders of the college chose one of their own, William Butterfield, as the architect, who proceeded to produce a riot of Victorian Gothic on a scale hitherto unseen. Contentious from the very beginning, Keble continues to attract its fair share of criticism. It was built not of Oxford stone, but of brick, and in addition to the dominant red, Butterfield used different colours to create his hallmark polychromatic patterning. Nowhere are the aspirations of the college's creators more evident than in the enormous **Chapel**, visited not generally for its kitschy mosaics and stained glass, but for Holman Hunt's famous painting *The Light of the World*, which hangs in a side chapel to the south.

Keble College

55

Just to the north of Keble, bright summer days in particular attract locals and visitors alike to the huge expanse of the ★ **University Parks** 76. Dotted with magnificent trees and shrubs and bordered on its eastern side by the River Cherwell, the park is a wonderful place for a stroll. It is also the home of the **Oxford University Cricket Club**, and this is one of only two places in England where first-class matches can be watched free of charge. If you're not there for the Australians or the Pakistanis, there may be a county fixture going on.

Cricket in the Parks

Opposite Keble is the impressive neo-Gothic facade of the ★★ **University Museum** 77 (Monday to Saturday noon–5pm). Supported by numerous progressive thinkers including John Ruskin, work began on this temple of natural history in 1855. The design was controversial at the time because the Gothic style was thought to be inappropriate for a secular structure, but there can be no denying the splendour of the interior. The central aisle of the main hall is dominated by the fine skeleton of an iguanodon, whose rib structure appears to be repeated in the wrought-iron vaulting of the glass roof. Slender iron columns divide the hall into three bays; the arcade columns around the sides are each hewn from a different British rock. Surrounding the hall are the statues of eminent sci-

University Museum

Pitt Rivers exhibits

entists, while further embellishment is provided by stone carvings of plants, birds and animals (created by the brothers O'Shea from Dublin). Apart from the dinosaurs, a famous attraction of the museum is the painting of the Dodo in the northwest corner of the building. The bird in question was brought to England in 1638 and formed part of the Tradescant and subsequently Ashmolean collections. It is well worth visiting the upper gallery for its fine collections of insects, butterflies and birds; there are also great views across the main hall.

If you're impressed by the University Museum, then you'll be staggered by what lies beyond, through the doors to the rear. The ★★★ **Pitt Rivers Museum of Ethnology** ⓲ (Monday to Saturday 1–4.30pm) was built in 1885 to house the collection of Lieutenant-General Augustus Henry Lane Pitt-Rivers, built up during his service in exotic lands with the Grenadier Guards. The original collection consisted of some 15,000 objects, but since then the number has swelled to well over a million, of which some 400,000 are on permanent display. The exotic exhibits come from all corners of the earth; in accordance with Pitt-Rivers' wishes, they are displayed not by region but by type, so model Chinese junks are to be found next to African dug-out canoes, etc. There is a cabinet containing the shrunken heads of Ecuadorian Indians, complete with instructions on head shrinking. Attendants will point out all kinds of other ghoulish delights.

The museum has an annex in the **Balfour Building** at 60 Banbury Road, which is also well worth visiting. It contains a **Hunters and Gatherers** section, describing the past and present from prehistoric axe-heads to Eskimos and Bushmen, as well as the ★ **Musical Instruments Collection**, with specimens from all over the world and again arranged according to type. Headsets are provided so that you can listen to the various types of music as you walk through the gallery. Concerts are held here in summer.

From Pitt Rivers return down Parks Road towards Broad Street. On the left is **Wadham College** ⓳. Built in 1609–13, it is the youngest of Oxford's pre-Victorian foundations. The **Front Quad** is distinguished by its fine Jacobean-Gothic portal, a scaled-down version of the Tower of the Five Orders in the Old Schools Quadrangle (*see Route 1, page 18*). The **Chapel** contains some fine stained glass including the magnificent east window by Bernard von Linge (1822), brother of the more famous Abraham. Beyond lies the wonderfully serene **Fellows' Garden**, the perfect environment in the 1650s for mathematicians and scientists such as Christopher Wren and Robert Boyle to meet up and discuss their theories, before moving on to London to found the Royal Society.

Wadham College hall

Port Meadow and beyond

*River Thames
and Port Meadow*

If you walk northwards along Walton Street (*see Route 8, page 52*) and then turn left down Walton Well Road, you'll come to a bridge which crosses the railway and canal and leads to one of Oxford's most beautiful and enduring treasures, the 400-acre (160-hectare) expanse of ★★★ **Port Meadow**.

Used continuously for grazing ever since its first mention in the Domesday Book (1087), the meadow is a rare piece of Old England; it has never once been ploughed over, and today, except for the winter months, visitors are still invariably outnumbered by horses and cattle. The meadow is also rich in birdlife and wild flowers; the low-lying parts are often flooded by the River Thames.

Visitors can wander all over the meadow as long as they don't pick the wild flowers. But a popular route starts by following the main path across to the **Thames**. At the first bridge, an arm of the river is used for mooring houseboats and leisure craft, and the bank is popular for children who want to feed the ducks, swans and geese at the other side. The Thames itself is crossed a little further upstream, and if you continue past the sailing club, a path on the left leads to the village of **Binsey**, with its popular pub, the Perch (*see Food and Drink, page 69*). To the north of Binsey, a narrow lane leads for about half a mile to the church of St Margaret, where the principal attraction is the ★**Treacle Well** described by the Doormouse at the Mad Hatter's Tea Party in Lewis Carroll's *Alice's Adventures in Wonderland*. The well is also associated with the story of St Frideswide, Oxford's patron saint. Her suitor, the King of Wessex, was struck blind when he tried to carry her away, but she agreed to cure him on condition that he leave her in peace. The well miraculously appeared and its waters restored the king's sight.

Treacle Well

Excursion

Woodstock and Blenheim Palace

A corner of Woodstock

Situated on the A44 eight miles (13km) northwest of Oxford, ★★ **Woodstock** is a small English country town with an attractive main street (Park Street) flanked by fine Georgian-fronted houses and a collection of pubs, cafés and boutiques. The town derived much of its former prosperity from glove-making; while all the factories in Woodstock itself are now closed, gloves are still made in surrounding villages and sold at the **Woodstock Glove Shop** at the side of the Town Hall. Also in Park Street, in Fletcher's House, is the ★ **Oxfordshire County Museum** (May to September, Tuesday to Saturday 10am–5pm, Sunday 2–5pm; October to April, Tuesday to Friday 10am–4pm, Saturday 10am–5pm, Sunday 2–5pm). It provides a fascinating overview of the history of Oxfordshire from the earliest times to the present day, with displays on archaeology, agriculture and domestic life. At the back is a pleasant garden with temporary exhibitions of contemporary sculpture.

Oxfordshire County Museum

Delightful though it is, Woodstock is somewhat overshadowed by its neighbour, the enormous ★★★ **Blenheim Palace** (house: 15 March to 31 October daily 10.30am–5.30pm; park: all year daily 9am–5pm). Reached either on foot through the archway at the end of Park Street, or by car through the gates at the entrance to the town, this is a true giant among English country houses. It was built by the nation for John Churchill, 1st Duke of Marlborough, in recognition of his great victory over the French at the Battle of Blenheim in 1704, and occupies the site of Woodstock's old Royal Manor which was demolished after the Civil War. Designed by Sir John Vanbrugh and

Blenheim Palace

his assistant Nicholas Hawksmoor, Blenheim is said to be a masterpiece of the English baroque style, although its ostentatious features and almost ruthless imposition on the English landscape, made it the object of controversy from the moment it was completed.

The attractions of the interior include the magnificent gilded ★★ **State Rooms**, adorned with an impressive array of tapestries, paintings, sculpture and fine furniture, and the beautiful ★ **Long Library,** which contains some 10,000 volumes and a Willis organ. It is easy to forget, looking at the scale of the palace, that it was actually built as a home. Sir Winston Churchill was born here in 1874, and his room provides the core of an ★ **exhibition of Chuchilliana**, including manuscripts, paintings, books, photographs and letters. Unlike the 1st Duke of Marlborough, who is commemorated by a large monument in the palace chapel, Sir Winston is buried in a simple grave in the parish church of Bladon on the southern periphery of the estate.

But many visitors to Blenheim never actually go inside the palace, preferring instead to explore the attractions of its enormous park. Covering some 2,100 acres (800 hectares), this was landscaped by 'Capability' Brown and includes as its centrepiece ★★ **Blenheim Lake**, which is spanned by Vanbrugh's Grand Bridge. The shallow side, the Queen Pool, is well worth strolling around; home to a large variety of water fowl, it is a popular place for birdwatchers. Visitors can also hire rowing boats and coarse fishing is possible.

In Blenheim's grounds

A further outdoor attraction is the ★★ **Marlborough Maze**, the world's largest symbolic hedge maze and an absolute must for visitors. It occupies the **Walled Garden** at the southern side of the estate, together with putting greens, giant chess and draughts and bouncy castles. This forms part of the **Pleasure Gardens** complex, which also includes a herb and lavender garden, butterfly house, cafeteria and adventure play area.

Also for the children, a **miniature railway** trundles across the parkland between the palace and the pleasure gardens. The alternative is to walk, admiring on the way the magnificent gnarled oak trees, many of which bear an almost uncanny resemblance to the *ents* in Tolkien's *Lord of the Rings*.

All aboard the miniature railway

Blenheim is obviously not the only major attraction within easy reach of Oxford. Away to the west are the Cotswolds, whose delightful villages and towns are described in our *Insight Compact Guide: The Cotswolds*. To the northwest are Warwick Castle and Shakespeare's town of Stratford-upon-Avon, both covered in the equally comprehensive *Insight Compact Guide: Shakespeare Country*.

Art and Architecture

Opposite: Christ Church Cathedral

Not much remains of Oxford's earliest architecture, the only surviving Saxon relic being the tower of the church of St Michael at the Northgate, which was built as a lookout tower against the advancing Danes. From the Norman era there is the fine crypt of St Peter in the East as well as St George's Tower, part of the castle. The abbeys which played such a pivotal role in establishing the city as a centre of learning were almost completely destroyed during the Reformation, although most of the Augustinian priory church built on the site of St Frideswide's priory was saved and subsequently became Christ Church Cathedral.

College blueprints

Oxford's principal architectural heritage has been endowed by the colleges and the university. Founded by rich and powerful bishops, Oxford's first medieval colleges were a stark contrast to the cramped academic halls in which most students lived and worked. Their creators could afford to construct fine buildings for the college members. Components included a chapel, a grand dining hall, accommodation set around an intimate quadrangle (much in the style of a medieval inn), a library to house the priceless manuscripts and, last but not least, a battlemented gatetower, designed to ward off unwanted visitors and to protect the college from the very real possibility of attack. While we can see the blueprint for some of these features in the surviving Mob Quad and chapel at Merton (*see Route 4, page 22*), it wasn't until the foundation of New College in 1379 (*see Route 2, page 31*) that all of them were combined for the first time into a unified whole, with the chapel and hall and library all occupying space within the main quadrangle. This general layout was repeated in most subsequent college foundations.

Merton Gate Tower

61

Medieval miracles

As the colleges grew, they either expanded or were in some cases completely rebuilt. Nevertheless, some fine examples of the medieval stone mason's art remain in Oxford, principally in the chapels. Though not part of a college at the time they were built, both the Latin Chapel and the Lady Chapel in Christ Church Cathedral are fine examples of the Early English style of Gothic architecture. With their pointed lancet windows and clusters of shafts in place of monolithic columns to support the vaulted roof, they are a marked contrast to the rather crude Norman nave.

Merton College Chapel demonstrates the transition that took place in the early 14th century to the Decorated style. With its flowing and curvaceous tracery, the chapel's huge east window is one of the finest examples in England.

Chapel window, Merton College

As the university grew in stature, it needed more of its own buildings, independent of the colleges. The first major step in this direction was the all-important Divinity School (*see Route 1, page 17*). Completed in 1488, it is a fine example of Perpendicular Gothic, with its intricate fan or lierne vaulting. Further examples of this form of vaulting include the Christ Church choir.

Later overlays

During the reign of Elizabeth I, college and university buildings began to dominate the central area. But the Elizabethan era and the first half of the 17th century also brought enormous changes to the town. Streets were extended and lined with three- and four-storey houses, mainly of timber-framed construction, of which several notable examples remain, including Kemp Hall just off the High Street (*see Route 5, page 34*). Medieval courtyard inns expanded to take up much space in the central streets; parts of such an inn remain in the Golden Cross off Cornmarket and The Mitre on High Street.

The 17th century also saw the emergence of Oxford's very own style of architecture, the Jacobean-Gothic, incorporating a tentative mixture of Gothic and Classical features and motifs and best exemplified by the magnificent Old Schools Quadrangle (*see Route 1, page 18*). But less than 100 years later, Classical architecture began to alter the Oxford skyline, with fine university buildings being erected in the central area, including Wren's Sheldonian Theatre (1668), Hawksmoor's Clarendon Building (1715) and Gibbs' Radcliffe Camera (1748).

Magnificent though they are, these buildings did not destroy the essentially medieval face of Oxford. Even when they were rebuilt, most colleges remained extremely conservative. The ancient-looking frontage of University College was completed at the same time as the Clarendon Building. Hawksmoor submitted plans for a neoclassical rebuild of All Souls, but these were not accepted; nor were the designs of Sir John Soane for Brasenose, whose medieval High Street facade was only completed in the early 20th century.

In the 19th century, Oxford was a bastion of Gothic Revivalism, apparent in the enormous chapel of Exeter College, built in 1854–60 by Sir George Gilbert Scott and almost an exact copy of Sainte Chapelle in Paris. Gothic forms and motifs were also used for secular buildings, the most notable example of which is the University Museum (1855). The founder of the Oxford Movement, John Keble, is remembered in Keble College, which was founded in 1868. William Butterfield's daring design transgressed Oxford's hallowed traditions, for it was built not of stone, but of a byzantine riot of red, yellow and blue brick.

Old Schools Quadrangle

Sheldonian Theatre

62

Brasenose College

The essential Oxford skyline of towers and spires has remained, but the architectural heritage of the city has been enriched by the construction of a number of fine modern buildings. These include the Sainsbury Building at Worcester College, which fits wonderfully into the parkland, the Beehive Buildings at St John's College, and the much-derided new Arco Building at Keble, which both blends in with its brick surroundings and sets new dynamic accents of its own.

Keble's Arco Building

Miracles of stone

Oxford is home to a profusion of architectural styles, and the fact that these appear to hang together so harmoniously is largely down to the local limestone of which most of the older buildings are constructed. Nowhere is the harmonising power of the Oxford stone more evident than in Radcliffe Square, whose buildings were all built at different times but nevertheless combine to form one of the most magnificent architectural ensembles in Europe. And if you cross the High Street, the facade of Brasenose College (19th–20th centuries), the spire of St Mary's (13th-century) and the portal of St Mary's (16th-century baroque) all appear to be part of the same intricate scheme.

63

Visitors should not just study the structure but also the details, particularly the gargoyles and string courses of sculptures lining the facades. Many of these are not as old as one might assume and spotting them is part of the fun of a stroll around the city. Spy the bespectacled librarian in the Old Schools Quadrangle or the rugby player on the High Street facade of Brasenose.

St Mary's Gargoyle

Stained glass

There are many fine examples of stained glass in Oxford, much of it, including the magnificent east window of Merton Chapel, the handiwork of local medieval craftsmen. But foreign artists, too, played their part, the most prolific being the German Abraham von Linge, who arrived in the city in 1629. His exquisite craftsmanship and intense colours can be admired in the chapel of The Queen's College, as well as at Lincoln and University.

Later contributions came from William Morris and Edward Burne-Jones, who met while studying at Exeter College in the 1850s. Influenced by the ideas of John Ruskin and the Pre-Raphaelites, together they devoted their lives to the revival of medieval arts and crafts, and their designs for fabrics, wallpaper, furniture, tapestries and stained glass revolutionised Victorian taste. Exeter College chapel houses one of their tapestries of the *Adoration of the Magi*, but it was in stained glass that they left their most notable mark on Oxford, particularly in the chapels and choir of Christ Church (*see Route 5, page 43*).

Burne-Jones window, Christ Church

Literature, Music and Theatre

Literature

Oxford has been home to numerous poets, novelists and playwrights. Some have praised it, some have scorned it, and others have simply drawn inspiration from it, such as Max Beerbohm with his satire of undergraduate life *Zuleika Dobson* (1911). But Oxford has been the setting of fantasy as well as fiction. Charles Dodgson, alias Lewis Carroll (1832–98), lived much of his adult life in Christ Church College. He was a shy, almost reclusive man, but nevertheless became acquainted with the daughters of the Dean and their friends. Details of *Alice's Adventures in Wonderland* are all over Oxford: the Cheshire Cat sat in the bough of the tree that still graces the Christ Church Deanery Garden; the Treacle Well is still at Binsey and 'the loveliest garden you ever saw' is at Worcester College. But the tale actually began with a boat trip along the river 'all in the golden afternoon' of 4 July 1862.

Inspiration for Lewis Carroll

J.R.R Tolkien (1898–1963), who studied at Exeter College, also found inspiration for *The Hobbit* and *The Lord of the Rings* in Oxford. Middle Earth can be found at the nature reserve out in the suburb of Risinghurst, but Tolkien must also have spent time in Blenheim Park, with its giant, contorted oak trees. C.S. Lewis (1898–1963) was also inspired at Risinghurst, for this is where he created his magical world of Narnia. Both writers met up with fellow members of the Inkling Group in the venerable Eagle and Child pub on St Giles *(see page 53)*.

Music and Theatre

Oxford is the home to many of England's finest professional musicians and you can enjoy classical concerts all the year round, especially during the Oxford Music Summer. Tickets are available at the Box Office of the Oxford Playhouse, Beaumont Street, tel: 01865 798600. The main concert venues are the Sheldonian Theatre, the Town Hall, the Holywell Music Room (the oldest purpose-built venue in the world) and the Jacqueline du Pré Music Building, but some of the city's churches as well as college chapels provide further fine settings for recitals and concerts.

Oxford boasts a lively theatrical tradition

The Apollo Theatre in George Street (tel: 01865 244544) provides a full range of theatrical activity for all tastes, including ballet, opera, drama, comedy and pantomime, as well as being a venue for pop and classical concerts. The other major theatre is the Oxford Playhouse on Beaumont Street (tel: 01865 798600), with modern theatre, music, dance, opera and a wide range of children's events. The Old Fire Station Arts Centre in George Street has acquired a reputation for innovative programming, not only in theatre but also in music and dance.

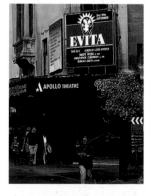

Calendar of Events

Encaenia Parade

Some events are geared to the Church or University calendar; information on precise dates can be obtained from the Oxford Information Centre (*see page 75*).

65

May
May Morning. Starts at 6am when Magdalen College Choir sings Latin grace from the Magdalen Tower. Followed by Morris Dancing in Radcliffe Square and Broad Street, as well as the more unorthodox practice of students jumping off Magdalen Bridge into the Cherwell.

Morris dancers

Ascension Day. Beating the Bounds. Starting at the church of St Michael at the Northgate, this is an ancient ceremony reconfirming the limits of St Michael's parish.

Eights Week. Held from the Wednesday to Saturday of the fifth week of Trinity (summer) term. Eight-oared crews from all colleges compete for the distinction of head of the river. The boat that crosses the finishing line without being bumped is the winner.

Spring Bank Holiday Monday. Lord Mayor's Parade of floats starting in St Giles and finishing at South Park.

Eights Week

June
Encaenia. Held on the first Wednesday in the week following the end of Trinity term. This is the main honorary degree ceremony. University dignitaries process to the Sheldonian Theatre.

September
St Giles' Fair. First Monday and Tuesday of the month. The origins of this colourful fair go back to a parish wake first recorded in 1624. The road is closed off to traffic and taken over by carousels old and new, shooting galleries, coconut shies and candy floss stalls.

Food and Drink

Oxford marmalade

As a city whose history has been dominated by the university, and which, apart from automobiles, has seen little in the way of home-grown industry, it comes as no surprise to learn that in food terms too, Oxford has hardly a single speciality of its own. The one enduring product, sold and universally recognised throughout the civilised world, is Frank Cooper's Oxford marmalade. No longer made in the city itself, the marmalade was first produced according to an old family recipe by Frank Cooper's wife, Sarah Jane, on her own kitchen range. In 1874, Frank started selling it in his grocery shop on the High Street, and the product never looked back.

If local food specialities have been somewhat thin on the ground in Oxford, this has traditionally been more than made up by liquid sustenance. Beer was brewed in Oxford ever since the first abbeys sprung up by the Thames and its myriad streams. The first brewery was established by the monks of Osney Abbey in Tidmarsh Lane, utilising the pure well water found deep beneath the river. The colleges tended to brew their own, and there was stiff competition to produce the strongest and tastiest ale. Back in the 1800s there were as many as 14 breweries located by the Castle Mill Stream and the canal. Today, there is not a single brewery left in Oxford, the last one, Morrells, having closed its gates in 1999.

As far as dining out is concerned, the cosmopolitan flavour of Oxford is reflected in the wide choice of cuisine offered by the numerous restaurants in the city and beyond. A key figure in putting this provincial English city on the international culinary map has been the renowned chef Raymond Blanc, with his award-winning Le Manoir Aux Quat'Saisons out at Great Milton and Le Petit Blanc restaurant in north Oxford; though the latter closed in 1989, the name is preserved in the Le Petit Blanc brasserie in Walton Street.

Raymond Blanc

Restaurants

£££ Expensive (over £60 for two); ££ Moderate (£30-60 for two); £ Inexpensive (under £30 for two).

Le Manoir Aux Quat'Saisons, Great Milton, tel: 01844 278881. Raymond Blanc ensures a unique but financially debilitating dining experience in his 14th-century manor house set in garden and parkland, 8 miles (13km) southeast of Oxford. Reservations essential. £££

Restaurant Elizabeth, 84 St Aldates, tel: 01865 242230. This small select restaurant with mainly French cuisine is probably the best in town, with prices to match. Reservations essential. £££

Le Petit Blanc

Gee's conservatory

Child-friendly Browns

Bath Place Hotel, 4/5 Bath Place, tel: 01865 791812. Award-winning restaurant in the hotel, serving 'modern European' dishes. Set luncheon and dinner menu which changes daily. Open to non-residents. £££

Shimla Pinks, 16 Turl Street, tel: 01865 245564. Award-winning Indian cuisine in tasteful modern décor. Specialises in Moghul cuisine. ££

Le Petit Blanc, 71–72 Walton Street, tel: 01865 510999. Raymond Blanc's latest venture in Oxford. Light but traditional French dishes in an airy atmosphere in young and lively Jericho – somewhere to eat well all day, including breakfast time. Decor by Terence Conran. ££

Gee's Brasserie, 61A Banbury Road, tel: 01865 553540. Well-established restaurant in the Raymond Blanc tradition in a beautiful, airy conservatory. ££

Luna Caprese Restaurant, 4 North Parade, tel: 01865 554812. Well-established restaurant serving classical Italian cuisine. Enthusiastic proprietor. ££

Browns, 5, 7, 9 & 11 Woodstock Road, tel: 01865 511995. This well-established restaurant offers breakfast, light lunches and three-course meals in a relaxed atmosphere. Open 11am–11.30pm. Advance booking only Monday to Friday, so expect queues at busy times. Children welcome. ££

Michel's Brasserie, 10 Little Clarendon Street, tel: 01865 552142. Regional French cuisine served seven days a week. Vegetarian menu available. ££

Café Français, 146 London Road, Headington, tel: 01865 762587. Nice bistro in Oxford suburb. ££

Cherwell Boathouse, Bardwell Road, tel: 01865 552746. Imaginative creations based on seasonal local produce in a beautiful location on the Cherwell. Complete the day out with a punt on the river. ££

Chiang Mai Kitchen, 130a High Street, tel: 01865 202233. Top-quality Thai cuisine at very reasonable prices in one of the finest 17th-century houses in the city, Kemp Hall. Special lunchtime menu. ££

Al-Shami, 25 Walton Crescent, tel: 01865 310066. Popular Lebanese restaurant serving Middle Eastern specialities. Quiet lunches, busy evenings. ££.

Opium Den Chinese Restaurant, 79 George Street, tel: 01865 248680. Authentic Chinese cuisine. £

Paddyfield Restaurant, 39 Hythe Bridge Street, tel: 01865 248835. Hong Kong-style Chinese food, specialising in lunchtime dim sum. £

The Polash, 25 Park End, tel: 01865 250244. Tandoori Restaurant, specialising in the cuisine of Madras. Situated opposite the railway station. £

Aziz Indian Cuisine, 230 Cowley Road, tel: 01865 794945. Bangladeshi cuisine on cosmopolitan Cowley Road. £.

Pizzeria Mama Mia, 8 South Parade, Summertown, tel: 01865-514141. Pleasant and long-established Italian restaurant, serving the best pizzas in Oxford. £.
Pizza Express, Golden Cross Walk, Cornmarket, tel: 01865 790442. The Golden Cross provides a pleasant setting for this branch of the popular pizzeria chain. £.

The Trout at Godstow

City pubs

For many, a visit to Oxford is not complete without sampling at least one of the city's delightful old pubs. These include the **Turf Tavern** between New College Lane and Holywell Street, which has a good selection of real ales and provides excellent buffet meals. Visitors can stay outside even in winter, keeping warm by the braziers. The **Eagle and Child** on St Giles is famous as the pub where the Inkling literary group (*see page 64*) used to meet up. **The King's Arms** on the corner of Parks Road and Holywell Street is popular with students and locals alike and has a good lunchtime buffet.

*Sign of the
Eagle and Child*

The King's Arms

Country pubs

There are a number of well-known pubs right on the city's doorstep. These include **The Perch** at Binsey, which has a large garden and excellent playground, though the food is overpriced. A short walk along the Thames brings you to the **Trout Inn** at Godstow. Situated right on the river, it has the added attraction of peacocks in the garden. The **White Hart** at Whytham near the western ring road has a pleasant garden in a very rural environment. A visit to **The Plough** at Wolvercote can be combined with a pleasant walk along the adjacent canal.

Those wishing to venture further afield in the county are recommended to buy the book *Pub Walks in Oxfordshire*, available from Blackwell's and other bookshops in the city.

Shopping

The main shopping thoroughfares in Oxford are **Cormarket Street** and **Queen Street**. This is where the chain stores are, such as Marks & Spencer, Bhs, Allders, Early Learning Centre, Gap, Next, Boots, WH Smith, HMV and Virgin Megastore etc.

Things are less hectic on **Broad Street**. This is where most of the bookshops are located, almost monopolised by the name of Blackwell. Blackwell's have always operated a policy of allowing shoppers to browse quite freely, and this is nowhere more enjoyable than at the main Blackwell's Bookshop at No 50, where there is a newly opened café on the first floor. The main competion to Blackwell's is provided by Waterstone's on the corner of Cormarket Street. Those interested in rare and second hand books might want to browse at Thorntons at No 11.

Though busy, **High Street** also has some interesting shops. Near the Oxford University Press Bookshop, Shepherd & Woodward at No 109–114 sells traditional menswear (including Barbour jackets), while Sanders of Oxford at 104 sells rare prints and maps. In Wheatsheaf Yard, behind No 128, is Gill & Co, Britain's oldest ironmongers, which goes back to 1530. Art collectors will be attracted by Oxford Gallery at No 23, while film enthusiasts can look in Vin Mag Co at No 50 for a postcard or poster of their favourite star.

Broad Street is connected to High Street by **Turl Street**, where there are a number of traditional shops, including Walters & Co at No 10, selling high-class menswear, and Past Times at No 4 selling historical gifts, including traditional games. Ducker & Son at No 6 sells high-quality handmade shoes.

Nearby is the wonderful **Covered Market**, whose traditional fishmongers and butchers hung with game now compete for the attention of shoppers with smart boutiques, florists, and upmarket delicatessens. On the way out to Cornmarket Street, Golden Cross Yard is home to all kinds of shops from souvenirs, model cars and jewellery to health foods and herbal remedies.

More interesting shops are found at **Gloucester Green**, where a general open-air market is held every Wednesday and an antiques and crafts market every Thursday. Beyond Gloucester Green, Walton Street, at the heart of trendy Jericho, has some interesting shops, particularly of the crafts and design variety. Exotic tastes are also catered for in Little Clarendon Street, which cuts through to St Giles. Here, Tumi Latin American Craft Centre sells jewellery, ceramics and clothing as well as a good choice of Latin American music. Ideal gifts for children can be found at Animal Animal just opposite.

Shop until you drop
Blackwell's Bookshop

Gloucester Green market

Waterways

Lazy day on the river

Oxford's three waterways, the Thames, the Cherwell and the canal provide a wonderful escape into rural surroundings right on the city's doorstep.

Probably the best place to see the Thames is at Port Meadow (*see page 57*). The walk along the river bank leads to the village of Binsey with its pub, the Perch, and continues all the way to the famous Trout at Godstow. Visitors can also enjoy the Thames at Christ Church Meadow and Folly Bridge, where the firm of Salters (tel: 243421) offers cruises along the river, both to the village of Iffley and to Abingdon. Iffley can also be reached by following the towpath; it is well worth visiting on account of the church of St Mary the Virgin, one of the most complete examples of the 12th-century Romanesque style in England. The interior of the Isis Tavern on the opposite bank is adorned with university boating regalia.

A popular way of exploring the peaceful backwaters of the Cherwell is by punt. Traditional Thames river craft, punts were originally used by the watermen for fishing and ferrying. Novices may have initial difficulties using the pole, but a paddle is supplied in case it gets stuck in the mud. Punts, together with rowing boats, may be hired from the Cherwell Boathouse, Bardwell Road (tel: 515978) and from C. Howard and Son at Magdalen Bridge (tel: 202643). The Cherwell can also be explored from dry land, notably the University Parks accessible from Parks Road and from Addison's Walk in the grounds of Magdalen College (*see Route 5, page 38*).

Last but not least is the canal, a busy industrial waterway after its completion in 1790, but now an oasis of tranquillity right on the edge of the city. The towpath walk from Hythe Bridge Street to the north is a delight at any time of year (*see Route 7, page 47*).

River Thames pleasure craft

Getting There

By plane

As well as the two major London airports, Heathrow (40 miles/64km) and Gatwick (70 miles/112km), Birmingham International Aiport (65 miles/104km from Oxford) handles direct flights from both Europe and the US, including British Airways flights from New York and American Airlines flights from Chicago. There are regular train connections from Birmingham to Oxford, as well as six coach services a day operated by National Express; the latter take 1 hour 30 minutes. From Heathrow, the Oxford Bus Company operates the the CityLink X70 coach service, which departs every half hour during the daytime and every two hours at night; the journey takes 1 hour 10 minutes. The CityLink X80 service from Gatwick runs every two hours and the journey time is 2 hours 10 minutes.

By car

From both London and the Midlands, Oxford is well served by the M40 motorway, which passes just to the north of the city. The journey from central London takes about 90 minutes, except during rush hour when it can take considerably longer to get out of the city along the A40 West Way. Drivers coming from London should exit at Junction 8, while those coming from the Midlands should turn off at Junction 9. If you're coming from either Gatwick or Heathrow airports, join the M40 via the London orbital motorway, the M25.

By bus

Services from London to Oxford's Gloucester Green Bus Station are very cheap and convenient. Stagecoach (tel: 01865 772250) operates the Oxford Tube, whose services depart London every 10 minutes from 9–10.30am and 15 minutes thereafter from Grosvenor Gardens (near Victoria Tube Station). CityLink X90 buses operated by the Oxford Bus Company (tel: 01865 785400) leave Victoria Coach Station every 20 minutes (15 minutes on Saturdays). Most journeys take about 1 hour 40 minutes, but during rush hour times you should allow for likely traffic congestion in London.

By train

There are frequent Great Western Intercity or Thames Trains services between London Paddington and Oxford. Trains depart every half hour during the morning and early evening, and hourly the rest of the day. Certain resticitions apply to travelling on Intercity trains, particularly during the early evening. For timetable information call the National Rail Enquiry Service, tel: 08457-484950).

73

High style motoring

An inexpensive option

Getting Around

By bus

Within central Oxford, both the Oxford Bus Company (CityLine, tel: 01865 785400) and Stagecoach (tel: 01865 772250) have services every 4 to 5 minutes. Both bus companies offer special day return tickets, family tickets, as well as travel cards with unlimited travel in the city. All tickets are purchased from the driver.

Regional Bus Services, including those to Woodstock for Blenheim Palace, operate from Gloucester Green Coach Station.

Parking

Parking in central Oxford is limited, and in residential areas you often need a resident's parking permit. There are large car parks at Hythe Bridge Street, Gloucester Green and St Clements (all pay and display) as well as multistorey car parks at Westgate and St Ebbe's. There is further pay and display parking either side of St Giles, but during the day it is difficult to find a place. Visitors should note that traffic wardens in Oxford are very vigilant. After 6pm, parking in the city centre is much easier.

If you want to avoid the problem of parking, take the Park and Ride Service. You can park your car fee of charge and then take the bus from the Pear Tree car park in the north (A34, A44, or A4260); the Redbridge car park in the south (A34 or A4074); Seacourt in the west (A40 or A420); or Thornhill in the east (A40 from London).

Take a taxi

Taxis

Taxi ranks are found at St Aldates, St Giles and at the railway station.
A.B.C. Taxis, tel: 01865 775577 or 770077
001 Taxis, tel: 01865 240000
Oxford City Taxis, tel: 01865 794000

Car rental

Avis, 1 Abbey Road, tel: 01865 249000
Budget, Osney Lane, tel: 01865 724884.
Vauxhall Car & Van Rental, City Motors, Woodstock Roundabout, tel: 01865 559955.
Ford Rent-a-Car, Hartwell Ford, Seacourt Tower, West Way, tel: 01865 380348.

Pedal power

Bike hire

Cycling is popular in Oxford and, as well as many cycleways, there are clear signs to enable cyclists to avoid the main streets. Bikes can be hired from Cycle King, 128–130, Cowley Road, tel: 01865-728262 and Bike Zone, 6 Lincoln House, Market Street, tel: 01865-728877.

Facts for the Visitor

Getting your bearings

Tourist Information

The Oxford Information Centre, the Old School, Gloucester Green, has a wealth of information on Oxford and the surrounding area, including a selection of maps and guide books. The centre also helps with accommodation and organises guided tours. Open Monday to Saturday 9.30am–5pm, Sunday only during the summer 10.30am–1pm, 1.30–3.30pm, tel: 01865 726871, fax: 01865-240261, (website www.oxfordcity.co.uk).

75

Cash dispensers and Link machines

Abbey National: Carfax
Barclays: Cornmarket Street
Lloyds: Broad Street, High Street
HSBC: Cornmarket Street, Clarendon Shopping Centre
National Westminster: Cornmarket Street, George Street
Royal Bank of Scotland: St Giles

Travel services

American Express Travel Services, 4 Queen Street, tel: 01865 792033

Sightseeing tours

There are guided walking tours leaving from the Oxford Information Centre, Gloucester Green, daily at 11am, 1pm and 2pm. There are also walking tours from Carfax Tower on Friday, Saturday and Sunday at 1.45pm. Both tours are led by members of the Oxford Guild of Guides. For information, tel: 01865 726871.

The Oxford Information Centre also organises special interest tours like C. S. Lewis and Lewis Carroll tour, Inspector Morse Walking Tours, spooky Ghost Tours, etc. Wheelchairs are welcome on all tours.

Join a guided tour

Open-top sightseeing tours are organised by Guide Friday and the Oxford Classic Tour. You can join the bus at several marked bus stops in the city. The ticket is valid all day and you can get off and on the buses at your leisure. Guide Friday (The Oxford Tour), tel: 01865 790522; Oxford Classic Tour, tel: 01235 819393.

Opening times

Some museums are closed on Mondays (Ashmolean, Museum of Modern Art, Museum of Oxford). Others are closed on Sundays (University Museum, Pitt Rivers, Museum of Oxford).

Most colleges are open to visitors in the afternoon only from 1 or 2 to 4 or 5pm. Brasenose is also open from 10–11.30am, Christ Church Monday to Saturday 9–5pm, Sunday 1–5pm; Magdalen daily 2–6pm; New College daily 11am–5pm; Trinity College daily 10.30am– noon and 2–5pm; St Edmund Hall daily from dawn till dusk. The Queen's College is only open to visitors on a tour booked at the Oxford Information Centre with the Oxford Guild of Guides. Visitors wishing to see Pembroke College are requested to enquire at the porter's lodge. University College, St. Cross College and Green College are generally closed to the public at all times.

Trinity is open more than most

Visitors should note that the above times can only be used as a guide. Colleges have the habit of closing, often for weeks on end, particularly during exam times but also as a result of building works or simply at the whim of the all-powerful porter.

Postal services

The main post office is in St Aldates, open Monday to Friday 9am–5.30pm, Saturday 9am-6pm. For help or advice on all counter services call the Customer Help Line, tel: 0845-722 3344.

Emergencies

Police, ambulance, fire brigade, tel: 999
Thames Valley Police, St Aldates, tel: 01865 266000
John Radcliffe Hospital, Headley Way, Headington, tel: 01865 741166

Help is at hand

Disabled access

The Oxford City Council has published a leaflet, *Oxford on the Level*, which is a self-guided walking tour for people using a wheelchair. This leaflet and a list of premises which are accessible to wheelchairs is available at the Oxford Information Centre, Gloucester Green. Free wheelchairs or scooters can be borrowed from Oxford Shopmobility, a scheme funded by the City Council. Booking is required, tel: 01865 744478.

Oxford for Children

In Oxford itself, children will be particularly fascinated by the **Pitt Rivers Museum** (*see page 56*), where they can ask the attendant to show them the giant toad or even the witch in a bottle. As well as the dinosaurs, the **University Museum** (*see page 55*) also has the portrait of the same Dodo that features in *Alice's Adventures in Wonderland*. Young visitors to the **Ashmolean Museum** (*see page 49*) will be enthralled by its large collection of Egyptian mummies as well as Powhattan's Mantle (Powhattan being the father of Pocahontas). Displays in the **Museum of Oxford** (*see page 40*) include some interesting finds from prehistoric times, as well as a large placard with a simplified version of the Legend of St Frideswide, the city's patron saint – good for young readers. **The Oxford Story** (*see page 26*) provides an unusual ride back in time to show the history of Oxford University; a special commentary for children is available.

For children who prefer to be outdoors, there are plenty of possibilities within easy reach of the city. **Shotover Country Park** beyond Headington is a delight for all those who like playing hide and seek and climbing trees; there is also a 'natural' sandpit for the younger ones. At **Port Meadow**, children will enjoy patting the horses and also feeding the ducks, geese and swans at the bridge over the Thames. To the north of the city, beyond the ring road, **Cutteslowe Park** has an aviary as well as a fine playground; on occasional Sundays hobby enthusiasts take children for rides around their miniature train circuit.

Ideal for a rainy day is a visit to **Wiz Kids**, 2nd floor, Threeway House, Gloucester Green (daily 10am–6pm, tel: 01865 791331). This is an indoor playground, where kids under the age of 8 can let off steam while mum and dad have a rest and a cup of tea in the cafeteria.

The environs of Oxford also have much to offer children. **Cotswold Wildlife Park** near Burford (daily 10am–6pm or dusk if earlier) is a half-hour drive from the city. Even before seeing the animals, children will probably demand a session in the adventure playground as well as a ride on the narrow gauge railway. A similar railway trundles through **Blenheim Park** (*see page 59*), which also has an adventure playground. At **Cogges Manor Farm Museum** in Witney children will be fascinated by the hand milking and butter-making, as well as crafts demonstrations held in the barn. Young steam buffs should be taken to the **Didcot Railway Centre** in Didcot (October to March, Saturday and Sunday 11am–5pm; April to September daily 11am–5pm, tel: 01235 817200). Telephone beforehand to enquire when the steam trains will be put through their paces.

High-chair view

The Oxford Story

Making friends on Port Meadow

Accommodation

Accommodation in Oxford is not cheap, and while there are plenty of bed and breakfasts, there is only a limited number of hotels. Booking ahead is therefore essential, especially in summer and on weekends. For visitors arriving in the city without accommodation, the Oxford Information Centre at Gloucester Green (*see page 75*) offers a room booking service for a small fee.

Old Parsonage Hotel

City

££££ (over £150 per night double)

Old Parsonage Hotel, 1 Banbury Road, tel: 01865 310210, fax: 311262. A fine and well-located hotel in the renovated old parsonage next to St Giles' church. Thirty luxuriously appointed en-suite bedrooms. The Parsonage Bar restaurant is open all day, also to non-residents. Excellent afternoon tea.

Randolph Hotel, Beaumont Street, tel: 01865 247481, fax: 791678 Oxford's most famous hotel is situated in the city centre, right opposite the Ashmolean Museum. There are two restaurants, the Spires Restaurant on the ground floor and the less formal Vaults Bistro in the basement; also two lounges, a coffee shop and bar. Extensive conference facilities.

£££ (over £95 per night double)

Cotswold Lodge Hotel, 66A Banbury Road, tel: 01865 512121, fax: 512490. Beautiful Victorian building, situated in quiet conservation area, only a few minutes walk from the city centre. Bar serving coffee and light meals, as well as restaurant serving lunch and dinner. There are also conference facilities.

Eastgate Hotel, 23 Merton Street, tel: 01865 248244, fax: 791681. Traditional hotel in a central location, adjacent to the site of Oxford's old East Gate and opposite the Examination Schools. Restaurant and bar.

Bath Place Hotel, 4–5 Bath Place, tel: 01865 791812, fax: 791834 Family-run hotel in the heart of Oxford occupying a group of restored 17th-century cottages. Excellent restaurant.

££ (over £70 per night double)

Parklands Hotel, 100 Banbury Road, tel: 01865 554374, fax: 559860. Small privately-owned hotel situated about half a mile (0.8km) north of the city centre. Mainly bed and breakfast accommodation but offering meals when required. Parking facilities.

Parklands Hotel

Victoria Hotel, 180 Abingdon Road, tel: 01865 724536, fax: 794909. Small, friendly hotel, within walking distance of the city.

The Old Black Horse Hotel, 102 St Clements, tel: 01865 244691, fax: 242771. Attractive hotel in a 17th-century building just across Magdalen Bridge. All rooms en-suite; restaurant and bar.

The Galaxie Hotel, 180 Banbury Road, Summertown, tel: 01865 515688; fax: 556824. Friendly, family-run hotel near the shopping and leisure facilities of the Summertown residential district.

Westgate Hotel, 1 Botley Road, tel: 01865 726721, fax: 722078. Very convenient for both the city (5 minutes walk) and the coach and railway stations. Restaurant and bar.

Palace Hotel, 250 Iffley Road, tel: 01865 727627, fax: 200478. Small hotel in a Victorian town house about 1 mile from the centre. Parking available.

Marlborough House Hotel, 321 Woodstock Road, tel: 01865 311321, fax: 515329. Small, luxurious hotel, situated in residential area about 1½ miles (2.4km) from city centre. Continental breakfast in bedrooms, which are all en-suite and have their own kitchenettes.

Pine Castle Hotel, 290/292 Iffley Road, tel: 01865 241497 fax: 727230. Small family-run hotel 1¼ miles (2km) from the centre. Personal service and licensed bar.

Galaxie Hotel

79

£ (under £70 double per night)

Cotswold House, 363 Banbury Road, tel and fax: 01865 310558. Highly commended bed and breakfast accommodation. Non-smoking.

Norham Guest House, 16 Norham Road, tel: 01865 515352; fax 793162. Situated in a traditional Victorian residence in a quiet part of North Oxford, close to University Parks and within 15 minutes' walk of the city centre. All rooms en-suite. Good restaurants nearby.

Cumnor Hotel, 76 Abingdon Road, Cumnor, tel: 01865 863098, fax: 862217. Comfort and convenience in village on the edge of the city. Individually furnished rooms and attractive garden.

Highfield West, 188 Cumnor Hill, tel: 01865 863007. Comfortable well-appointed bed and breakfast accommodation in a residential area for around £50 a double. Mostly en-suite facilities. Outdoor pool in season.

Country
£££
Weston Manor, Weston on the Green, tel: 01869 350621, fax: 350901. 16th-century manor house set in beautiful gardens. Excellent cuisine in the Baronial Hall.

£
The King's Arms Hotel, Horton-Cum-Studley, tel: 01865 351235, fax: 351721. Country hotel offering rural peace, yet close to Oxford. Restaurant and lounge bar.

Index